Take That

How to Recognize and Repel Nonsense

· · · · · · · · ·

Jodie Eckleberry-Hunt, Ph.D., ABPP

©Jodie Eckleberry-Hunt, Ph.D., ABPP, PLLC
Jodieeckleberryhunt.com
ISBN 979-8-9986647-0-0

Table of Contents

Introduction..7

Boundaries 101 12

Reprogram Those Boundaries..27

Put the Brakes on Self-Sabotage....................................30

Focus on You 36

Fuck *I Can't* Thinking 40

And On to the Next Thing 42

Temper Tantrums While Driving.....................................47

Fear: The Vine That Chokes...50

Say, "No" to the Emotional Self......................................55

Self-Deprecation Is Abuse...59

Speech Therapy for Saying, "No" 61

Who the Hell Are You? (The Pursuit of Perfection) 63

Self-Improvement 68

There Are No Awards for Martyrs....................................72

The Self-Blame Factor...75

Worry Is Worshipping the Problem..................................80

Hit the Pause Button When You're Offended 82

The Throne of Self-Judgment...87

Enough with the Guilt...90

Cancer in the Mind...94

Horror Stories We Tell Ourselves....................................97

Imposter No More...100

Praise and Glory..104

All that Stuff 107

Negativity...111

Positivity 113

The Rearview Mirror 115

No Need to Look into the Crystal Ball 118

How Awful...120

You Are Enough 122

Don't Take the Bait..126

No One Wants to Hear That...................................128

Helping and the Fuck Budget 131

Your Good Intentions 133

Trips to Fantasy Land 138

That's Not Okay..142

The Knife in the Back 145

Parents Give, Kids Take—Rinse, Pause, Repeat? 149

Enabling Only Works with the Unable.......................152

Family Drama Is Baked In....................................157

Yes, Love Has a Boundary, Too...............................160

Fido Knows Exactly What He's Doing 163

You Do You..165

A Special Kind of Pain: Teenagers...........................171

Healthy Competition or Rivalry?.............................177

Attention Seeking..181

Oversharing..184

Stirring the Pot 186

In Fact, Ditch the Drama...189

Peacemaking or Distress Intolerance? 192

The Company You Keep 195

Can't Touch This 198

Gossip 202

Why Buy the Cow When You Can Get the Milk for Free?
....205

Check Your Political Agitation at the Door....................208

Take off the Social Handcuffs 212

Keeping Up with the Joneses...215

Fuck the Influencers..219

People-Pleasing and the Road to Nowhere......................223

The Truth About Work 227

Bonus Section: Expert's Guide to Setting a Boundary at
Work 231

Incivility—The Pig in Slop..234

Threats to Humanity 237

Non-Acceptance of Reality..242

Manipulation..245

Growth Robbery...247

Givers Attract Takers..250

Say, "No" to Numbing...255

Accept Conflicting Emotions...258

You Already Know What's in the News, and It Sucks....261

Social Media Is a Mindfuck...264

Time Is THE Most Precious Resource............................268

Money Won't Buy Happiness...273

Don't Pathologize Normal 278

The Bullshit Ends Here...283

Power and Control Are Illusions.....................................288

Do You See a Victim or Survivor? 292

Get Your Face Off the Screen...295

It's Time to Break Tradition 297

Health, Hypochondriasis, and Throwing in the Towel 300

Too Much of a Good Thing 305

The Pity Party 308

A Lonely Place Called Pride...311

Quick Fixes and Other Half-Assed Solutions 314

Too Much Empathy Is Self-Destructive 317

I Hear You...320

Assholery 323

Group Think Is Yesterday and Boring.............................326

Just Do It...328

The Outside Package...331

Labeling Is for the Post Office..333

When We Know How the Story Ends 337

Why Not Just Be Aggressive? 340

Understanding and Other Rabbit Holes 343

Money, Gifts, and Loans...346

Let's Get Real 349

Light That Bitch on Fire 351

The Last Word 354

The End...357

References...360

Introduction

This book is about boundaries because it is boundaries that help you recognize and repel the nonsense. But words are not enough. One-time action is not enough. Repelling absurdity takes significant, long-term mindset transformation and intentional, ongoing action. Understand there will also be backlash.

The word *boundaries* generates big talk in social circles and on our favorite entertainment programs. Setting boundaries sounds so empowering and healthy, but it is easy to minimize the effort and anxiety involved. Do you really understand the depth, scope, and work involved in creating them? Boundaries are so much more nuanced and complex than the pop-psychology trend suggests.

Boundaries are deliberate limits. They are internal and external; they are attitudinal. They involve awareness, confidence, and a sense of legitimacy and worth. It is too easy to use the word boundaries without fully comprehending how multi-faceted they are, and this is where folks struggle. Big talk without big action undermines success.

Myth: Setting boundaries is simply blocking out things you don't want to hear.

Truth: Nothing about setting boundaries is simple, and the only way to block what you   don't want to hear is to wall yourself off from the entire world. It's not even possible.

Myth: Boundaries are selfish.

Truth: Boundaries are about self-preservation; they are the ultimate self-care.

Accusations of selfishness are often leveled by those who want to control you.

Myth: If you set boundaries, people have to respect them.

Truth: Have you observed society lately? Respect is optional. The only person you can control is yourself. You can't make other people do anything. Boundaries target your actions, not those of others.

Get the complexity?

I'm here to break it down from a professional and human level, to take a deep dive into the broad scope of boundaries—how, when, and where to set them, and how to be prepared for people around you to push back. It's as predictable as taxes.

People have the right to be themselves. I understand and support that. I just don't believe that I am (or you are) required to be around their shenanigans and attention-seeking, misbehaving nonsense. This is a boundary. It isn't about imposing one's will on someone else. It is honest communication when your preferences conflict with someone else's, and if a compromise cannot be reached, you remove yourself from the situation. Clear messaging and your behavior are the elements you can control. You set those expectations.

People have the right to act badly, and they will. You, however, don't have to watch, listen, or experience the bad behavior. You can protect yourself with boundaries by validly expressing your needs and preferences and allowing others to express theirs. Have zero shame, guilt, or doubt in telling folks, "Take that shit over there," so they can continue without you being affected.

The goal of this book is to look at the concept of boundaries in a variety of interesting—perhaps previously unconsidered bite-sized situations. It is a tool to help folks reflect on how they may be leaving themselves open or vulnerable to being taken advantage of. Some of us are just inexperienced at boundaries because we were never taught to set them or taught that doing so makes us feel mean, rude, or selfish. Others may be good in one domain (like work) but bad in another (like family) due to emotional conditioning.

Why is this important? Because boundaries are the ultimate self-care and self-preservation tool. This book should serve to remind you that you control your boundaries and help you understand more about where they come from and why they are essential to health and wellness. As I tend to do, I will throw in some spicy language to get a smile of recognition, and I will repeat some lessons in case you missed it the first time around.

How did I come up with this guide? I've spent almost three decades studying people. This is what you have told me you struggle with and what I struggle with in the shitshow of life. I will give you lots of personal examples to demonstrate how deeply I get it. Ready to dive in? Read on, my friend.

Boundaries 101

What are boundaries exactly? They are personal restrictions or lines that you set to protect your physical and mental health based on your needs, wants, and preferences. Maybe I have a boundary that I won't answer a knock on my door unless I've received a call that visitors are coming because I prefer not to receive surprise company. Surprise guests disrupt my plans and feel intrusive. Note that this boundary does not require other people to do anything. People can call or not call. I am focused on how I handle what other people do.

Let's look at another example. I use skin as an example because it is universal, and most of us take it for granted. Your skin is a boundary, the first line of defense against foreign invaders. Maybe you have never given thought to what your skin does for you each and every day: Skin protects the rest of your body from anything that wants to get inside. Even if we aren't aware of what our skin is doing for us, it serves as a primary source of protection against friction, cuts, burns, and invaders.

We need some boundaries, even if we are not aware that we need them. I'm guessing that when you think of a boundary, you think of an intentional limit-setting, and this is correct. But what happens if we don't recognize a crucial time to set boundaries? What if we don't know when and where we need to set them?

Going back to the skin example, our skin serves as a primary source of protection even if we aren't always aware of what it is doing for us. Our skin is willing to roughen and callous up to keep us safe.

Thanks, skin, for always being there! (Aside: That's another reason to take good care of your skin.)

I am giving you a guide to think of boundaries across life domains and feel empowered to protect yourself. Think about it: You don't give your skin the day off. Maybe you put lotion on it. Maybe you cover it up. I am sure you sanitize and wash it. Some of us try to make it look younger and more resilient, especially as we age and get wise to what is going on.

Let's move on to expanding that wisdom.

Nuances of Boundaries

Boundaries, as limits, may be applied externally (with others) and internally (with self). You may find it surprising that you can and should set boundaries with yourself. Consider the times when you sit in self-judgment as your own worst critic to the point that it is crippling or self-defeating or when you need to give yourself permission to not please other people.

Boundaries are multi-faceted, multi-layered, interpersonal, and intrapersonal. The key to effective boundary setting is understanding the who, what, where, and why so you can properly match your strategy to the situation, resulting in maximally efficient bullshit-repelling properties.

While most people think of boundaries as verbal, they can also be non-verbal, such as *resting bitch face*, where you use your body and facial expressions to communicate a lack of interest in engaging in certain bullshit. In addition, boundaries can also be action-oriented, such as when you walk away from or otherwise end an unhelpful or toxic interaction.

Here's an illustration. Val was recently diagnosed with cancer and became overwhelmed with treatment options and decision-making. What wasn't helpful was that Val had a large social circle who freely gave her advice on what she should do. While this was intended to be helpful, Val was easily triggered by their second-guessing what she needed. I told her to share with her network that she would prefer not to hear their opinions, but she struggled to find the words. One day, she was telling a friend about something she was considering doing, and the friend launched into why that wasn't a good choice. Val lifted two fingers and said, "*Mmmmmm,*" and the conversation stopped. It was a perfect nonverbal limit. Nothing else was needed.

Verbal boundaries mean using words or language to indicate limit-setting. A person might, for example, say, "I'm not going to engage in this discussion," or "I don't want to be around you when you do or say these things." A person might outline preferences such as, "I need some time alone," "I don't want to go on Friday," or just "No." A more direct and less subtle approach might include the words: "Fuck off," "Shut the fuck up," or "Leave me the fuck alone." The choice of verb will depend on preference.

Let's call this the art of boundaries. There is the general technique, and you design or tailor it to your personality and creative taste. You are the artist. Keep in mind, though, that the best approach to choosing a particular boundary, in addition to your comfort level, involves understanding what the recipient will understand within that context. I use a tone-of-voice boundary with my family and the dog, and let's just say that they are capable of learning fast.

Self-Permission Is Perhaps the Hardest Part

A lot of people struggle with boundaries because they are unfamiliar or uncomfortable. Maybe you have been manipulated to believe that boundaries are selfish because you are saying, "No" to someone who wants you to do something for them. You may have been shamed into believing that boundaries are narcissistic because they don't serve someone else's purpose or convenience. I am a board-certified mental health professional, and I am telling you that boundaries are healthy and absolutely necessary for health, wellness, and survival. They are also essential for living a life that aligns with your values. More and more, this out-of-control world will take all you have and more if you allow it.

Sometimes, we stop and look at our lives and wonder how we got into such messed-up situations. First clue: It didn't happen overnight. Many people are not aware that much of the programming around boundaries happens when we are kids. Think of a two-year-old who goes around saying, "No," like it's the newest toy. Then, at some point, it seems we forget how to use the word at all, particularly if you identify as cis female.

Some of our first lessons around boundaries are learned by watching parents and caregivers. We mimic what these important people do, and we learn from what they teach us. If they empower us to stand up for ourselves, we learn to be assertive. If they teach us to please others, we learn to be self-deniers.

Question: Did you learn that "No" was a bad word? Did you learn that saying, "No" was acceptable or unacceptable? Think about that for a minute. How did important adults in your life respond to early boundary-setting experiments and assertiveness?

If you were sexually assaulted, molested, or violated, you may have learned that people are capable of invading even your most sacred space—your body—even if you say, "No." You may have learned that people you trust hurt you. You may have learned to feel as if you had no power.

If your efforts to put your needs first were shamed, you may have learned that boundaries are bad, selfish, or wrong. Women are especially susceptible to this, as our moms, too, struggled with always serving others first. Just because a behavior was normalized doesn't make it healthy. It is simply a perpetuated, self-defeating cycle.

If you learned that no does not mean no, you may have learned to give up the power of boundaries.

When I talk with folks in my office about boundaries, I typically get one of two reactions. The first is resonance. People heartily agree that they need to improve their boundaries but have no clue where or how to start. They understand boundaries in theory, but the practice part trips them up. This is normal in any behavior change. The second reaction is confusion, as if they have never heard of boundaries. Curiously, it is the second group that tends to take the idea of boundaries and run with it. They were just unaware of the concept.

You may be wondering what happens if you didn't learn healthy boundaries as you were growing and developing. Many of us didn't, and that is okay because you can learn them now, though it is harder and takes intentionality, as well as high pain tolerance. Creating your own space for individuality, self-protection, and peace, as in adolescence, can be something others around you don't understand or aren't familiar with. Expect pushback, which can be painful.

Here is a helpful hint to keep in mind throughout life: We are all works in progress. If we are doing this thing called life right, we will continue to grow until death. Give yourself a break. When others don't understand, that doesn't make it wrong. Your task is to find what you want and what makes you happy, and if others don't want that for you, that is their problem. It is important not to measure your success by others' reactions. It's like measuring height with a thermometer or tracking direction with a tape measure. How will you know where true north lies unless you recalibrate?

Boundaries are life preservers. They are meant to keep you afloat. Ships cannot sail without them for a good reason: They save lives. Make sure you are well-prepared. Be thoughtful about your limits so that when the waves begin to obscure your vision, you are able to hang on until they subside.

The most sane act possible is to survive.

A New Norm

With practice, boundaries can become part of your identity or how others know you. People may come to understand the things you will and won't tolerate, and those who respect your boundaries will honor them without you even having to invoke them. For example, if you love to host parties and do so often, those invited learn to ask you what you want them to bring (after you tell them all to stop bringing dessert) instead of automatically bringing crap you don't need or want.

This is the absolute splendor of boundary setting. Once put into practice, boundaries start to repel bullshit the way housework drives away teenagers. The beauty of setting boundaries is immediate self-protection, but there is the added benefit of creating norms for those around you to learn to adhere to.

Voilà! You have just cut the bullshit in your life in half. That's good for you and the environment. You're welcome.

Two Caveats

Remember, setting boundaries is about you, not about the other person or people. Be wary of making boundary-setting a commentary on others' behavior instead of simple ownership of your limits and preferences. Boundaries are not meant to control other people. If you find that you are talking about your boundaries but are focused on labeling someone else, it may be that you have forgotten about your own self-care. Remember that you cannot control others, and you shouldn't fixate on labeling and reacting to them, either. Boundaries are enhanced awareness and commitments around *your* needs and limitations.

The second caveat is that working on boundaries is a lifetime commitment because, as humans, we constantly grow and change—and so do our social settings. Some people may be disappointed that I don't give a how-to recipe or playbook in regard to setting boundaries. That is because it isn't straightforward and depends on the circumstances. No book can tailor-make guidance for every individual, despite the appeal of such a claim. Boundary-setting is more about being self-aware, self-understanding, and mindful, alongside a willingness to self-protect by limit-setting. In other words, it is a journey that will continue to develop.

The tools you need for this journey include understanding genetics and early life experiences, being self-reflective about emotional responses, catching and arguing with unhelpful self-talk, and being persistent about changing behavior. I have written about these techniques extensively in my other books and will not rehash that here. I will throw in some tools along the way, but if you want to learn more, I strongly recommend counseling to drill down into what is giving you the most trouble. There is no book that will make boundary-setting easy because humans are pleasing and social by nature. If that is what you seek, you will be looking for a long while. The work will be hard, but it will get easier. My hope is to feed your growth process and be provocative along the way. In other words, I want to get you thinking and experimenting. You do the rest.

I've tried to organize my suggestions on recognizing and repelling nonsense into themes, but let's be honest: Everything I talk about concerns you and involves others. Maybe it is more accurate to say that I impose some rather arbitrary groupings on topics to organize your reading experience. Each boundary could just as easily fit into other categories. After multiple revisions, I set a boundary with myself: It is what it is.

BOUNDARIES AROUND SELF-INFLICTED PAIN

Reprogram Those Boundaries

Mildred was the youngest in her family, and others were always touching her. They tickled her. They hugged her. They messed her hair. Sometimes, her siblings bullied her and said it was their right as the older kids. They hit her when her mom wasn't around. As Mildred grew older, she began to tell her family, "No," but they ignored her. They told her that she didn't get a say as the youngest. They walked into her room without knocking, even when she was dressing. They poked at her breasts when she was going through puberty, and they teased her. Mildred insisted that they stop, and she cried sometimes. Her parents didn't enforce her wishes and just laughed at what they saw as good-natured fun. When Mildred started working as an office assistant, she was uncomfortable with men in the office who were a bit too friendly and touched her in ways that she preferred they didn't. Mildred didn't say anything to these men because she thought it was just how the world worked. She sucked it up. She didn't want to come off as *bitchy*.

While our struggle with setting boundaries often begins with early learning, there is also an element of genetics. Folks who are born worriers or have social anxiety are genetically programmed to feel insecure or are excessively worried about what others are thinking. In these cases, boundary setting may be challenging for fear of judgment, shame, or rejection. Not everything can be blamed on our parents!

Regardless of why we struggle with boundaries, the solution is the same: behavior change. What I mean by that is that we have to change what we are doing regardless of why we are doing it that way. The behavior change comes first because we may never fully understand the why, and it can take years to see that light anyway.

Mildred deserved to work in a safe environment where she wasn't on the receiving end of unwanted touch.

She had every right to tell others to stop touching her. The work to be done was within Mildred—recognizing the early mistaken programming and granting self-permission to set limits.

In summary, whether our understanding of boundaries is shaped by flawed learning or genetics, it is important to recognize that our sense of boundaries may be skewed in favor of other people. This means that we may put our own needs behind our perceptions (which may, in fact, be inaccurate) of other people's wants. This is backwards. We may be acting on bad information, bad programming, or unfortunate genetics. It is always good to stop and question our brainwashing—our perspective—to see how it is working for us and if it is valid.

Time to update the operating system.

Put the Brakes on Self-Sabotage

The brain is hard-wired to self-criticize as a performance-enhancing quality control, but it only goes so far before it inflicts as much damage as it does benefits. The idea is that if we are constantly critiquing our performance, it offers the opportunity to continually improve. That's a great thing, right? Until it's not.

When people, because of genetics or early life experiences, tend toward perfectionism or outright self-abuse, they can be cruel in critiquing themselves. If they lean toward over-responsibility, they may beat themselves up for things that aren't even under their control. As with most things in life, how we go about self-critique is super important. Self-sabotage refers to the self-abuse—when the critiquing goes too far and is destructive to the self-image or self-esteem.

When something doesn't go according to plan in your life or doesn't work out or you make a mistake, do you automatically start telling yourself these things? *You are such a failure; look how dumb you are, you suck. Why do you even try? This is terrible; things will never work out.* This is self-sabotaging self-talk. It is rude, nasty, hateful, and hopefully, it isn't how you would talk to a friend, family member, or coworker. It also isn't how you should talk to yourself because it makes it more likely that you will fumble going forward since you are no longer just focused on what you need to do; you are carrying the weight of the condemnation. Plus, you've told yourself that you don't have the necessary requirements to succeed anyway, so why try?

I am very open about my generalized anxiety disorder (GAD). Folks who have GAD have minds that never stop. We are always preoccupied with what others think of us when they aren't thinking of us at all. We feel guilty for no identifiable reason and compelled to right a wrong even when we don't know what it is. We often feel insecure, restless, and agitated and don't know why. There is an endless loop of *what-if* thinking involving everything from health crises to school shootings to having control down to the minute of your daily schedule.

My self-sabotage statements tend to revolve around telling myself that someone is mad at me. I don't have to have any legitimate reason for thinking this. Perhaps it is someone who hasn't responded within a day to an email or text. It could be someone I haven't heard from in a while. It could be the mood I woke up in and the first person who popped into my mind. My anxiety hates tolerating the idea that someone could be mad at me and not knowing who or why, so I seem to randomly choose someone. I then create a reason as to why I *must* have offended the person. I ruminate on this until I have chewed off the skin around all of my nails, and then I make a plan to reach out and apologize for some imagined wrongdoing.

This is self-sabotaging because it is a needless waste of time, and it makes me look more than a little unbalanced. I can, in fact, lose the better part of a day worrying about nothing topped off by emotional eating that makes my body feel all nasty. This is incredibly wasteful and torturesome. I could have used the time on much more productive activities, as well as avoiding the headache I inevitably have as a result.

If I were talking to a friend or trusted family member who was telling me all of this, I would say to that person, "What is the evidence? If there is no evidence, this is your anxiety talking. You need to work to let it go in a healthy way." Yet, somehow, I have let the feeling take over, and the feeling is out of control. I am much better at distracting myself these days; it is a matter of awareness, reflection, and having a plan in advance. *Oh yeah, there it is. Breathe. Now, get busy with something different than this thought.*

When you note the barrage of negative self-evaluative comments, you need to intentionally step in to subvert the sabotage. Argue back. Ask yourself how any of the commentary is helpful. Ask yourself if this is how you would talk to someone you love. You can distract yourself. Even more, go look in the mirror, into your own human eyes, and find some self-compassion. You are, in fact, a human *being*. Take a deep breath. Go for a walk. Do something kind for yourself even if you made a mistake. Imagine what you might say to someone you love.

Set boundaries with your self-sabotaging self-talk. It will take practice to catch it as it is happening. It will take experimentation and practice to figure out what works best for you. Is it visualization, deep breathing, counterstatements, distraction, exercise, journaling, or talking to a friend? The commitment is recognition that beating yourself up is not productive and will not lead to the outcomes you desire.

The ultimate antidote for self-sabotage is self-compassion and mentorship—the kind of gentle guidance you would give someone you love. Come alongside yourself. Pick yourself up. Give yourself a hug. Move on.

Focus on You

Despite what you may have heard, boundaries are not just about saying, "No." Boundaries are also about giving permission. You can give yourself clearance to stop intervening in the lives of others under the false premise of *helping*. Boundaries are as much about agreeing to stay out of other people's business as they are about asking others to leave you alone. They are an acceptance of individuality without feeling the need to get involved or fix someone.

Lucille loves to help others even without being asked. In fact, she enjoys stepping in to give helpful advice or assistance before others even have to think of reaching out. Lucille particularly loves to solve others' problems with counseling. She has made some real doozy mistakes, and if she can help someone else, why wouldn't she? The problem is that sometimes Lucille's friends feel judged. They don't always want to tell her what is going on because they know what she will say before she even says it.

In this context, boundaries can be seen in two ways. First, they can take the form of Lucille telling herself she shouldn't get involved. She would certainly feel guilty about this, as if she is holding out when she *could be* helping. Another way to look at boundaries is Lucille telling herself it is okay or perhaps even more beneficial not to get involved because she may interfere with the other person's growth or learning process. If Lucille steps in, she may be imposing her values on someone else when things might have gone a very different way. That different way can be okay, even if Lucille doesn't agree with it.

Perhaps you never considered that two very different ideas, experiences, personalities, or styles can coexist without one changing or bending to accommodate the other. Boundaries are about allowing differences to exist—even if we find them embarrassing in people we love—without trying to alter the differences because they aren't ours to change.

My kids can dress and wear their hair in some ways that I find to be extra creative and attention-getting, but I don't have to impose my clothing preferences on them. I am sure they feel the same about me. They are not extensions of me nor I of them, and we can coexist without changing each other or taking responsibility for each other's decisions.

This is an important concept because we are giving ourselves freedom—freedom from the obligation, guilt, burden, and pain that come with feeling we should fix, enlighten, help, or change people we love.

Boundaries are permission to focus on our own shit. It doesn't mean we don't or won't care about others. It just means we respect other's self-determination in their own lives, and now we are welcome to work on ourselves. You do you, and others do themselves. We can't know what is best for them anyway, even if we *think* we do.

The focal point here is that the way we frame boundaries has a significant influence on how we set and react to them. Are we telling ourselves that we are being indifferent or selfish, or are we telling ourselves that we are being mature, accepting, and tolerant? Which person do you want to be?

Fuck *I Can't* Thinking

Fuck *I can't* thinking. It is a negative bias or mindset that most likely is untrue. I cannot emphasize enough how much people hate my reaction when they say, "I can't," in my office. I keep interrupting with, "Haven't learned how to yet." *Can't* means you don't have the ability. I don't have the ability to play pro basketball and am five feet tall in my fifth decade, so yeah, I probably can't play pro ball. You *can* set boundaries. You *can* get out of your comfort zone. You *can* do new things.

Many of the things that we tell ourselves we *can't* are more appropriately labeled *we'd prefer not to*—for example, "I can't say no." Well, unless your mouth doesn't work, you *can*. You prefer or choose not to. We *can't* say how we feel. No, we may be afraid or don't know the best words, but we can. We *can't* set boundaries. Again, it is more likely that we mean we have not yet learned how to do so in a way that feels comfortable. Waiting for comfort is like waiting to win the lottery. You're probably going to be waiting a very long time. We are often waiting to discover a miraculous way to set boundaries that doesn't feel like setting boundaries.

Catch the *I can't* and hold yourself accountable. Remember, you are not a victim. You are a survivor working on being a thriver. Get to know your internal badass and start with *I will*.

And On to the Next Thing

Martin Seligman is considered by many to be the father of positive psychology. [1] He spent many years studying the origins of depression before moving on to study happiness. Seligman proposes the term *hedonic treadmill* to describe something most of us do that undermines happiness.

Let's say that you are living life, and you feel that something is missing. It's a car. If you had this perfect car, your life would be so much more complete. You are sure that having a nice car will make you happy. So, you get a new car, and it is glorious… For a while. Then, you get an itch for something else. Perhaps you think, "Wow, I need a new entertainment center with the latest tech to make home a nice place to hang when I am not driving my car." So, you build your entertainment center, and that lifts your mood significantly for a while, although not quite as long as the car. *Hmmmm.* You now notice that your apartment stands out like a sore thumb in comparison to your car and entertainment center. You start to feel down and incomplete, telling yourself that you just need a new condo to make it all work.

It may sound like I am just talking about the accumulation of things (which I will get to a bit later), but it is more complex than that. I am talking about an obsessive focus on the next best things in life. It may be the next best job, the next best adventure, the next best life partner. The hedonic treadmill refers to the insatiable quest for better, which is so consuming that you don't appreciate what you have and where you are in the present moment.

Initially, you are walking on the treadmill and building the life you want, but each time you get something, you want more. The highs don't last as long each time you move on to something new, and before you know it, you are running on the treadmill chasing the next thing. There may be as much running from allowing the disappointment to sink in as there is from getting the next buzz.

Don't get me wrong, wanting improvements isn't a bad thing. What is not so good is a lack of appreciation for the here and now—what you have. When there is too much emphasis on the future and telling oneself that things will be better "when" ("In order to be happy, I just need…"), the problem is that the cycle doesn't end, and there is no sense of satisfaction.

I have had people tell me that because they have worked so hard for so long, they have a difficult time enjoying vacation. They feel they need to be doing something more; they just can't let go. Ever had that feeling? It's a bit unsettling to be somewhere beautiful and feel it isn't enough when your head is telling you it should be. Chasing the next best thing can be like that. My suggestion for folks in the above situation is to practice just being. Retrain the brain to not multi-task or feel something is missing. It takes a bit of practice, but it can be done. The brain is naturally vulnerable in this way, so it isn't that there is something wrong if this describes you. You just have to work equally hard to remind yourself that happiness isn't going to be found external to you (unless you don't have safety, food, water, shelter, etc.). Happiness is found within. It is appreciating peace. It is appreciating the moment. Happiness is fighting the lies that say, "It's over there!" Happiness isn't a matter of leaving *here* and going *there*. *There* just comes with another set of problems. Instead, happiness is about learning to master the problems in front of you. It is also about understanding the meaning of satisfaction, which is probably a great synonym for happiness. The highs include joy and should be appreciated. However, you need to understand that joy is not a permanent state. If every moment was peak, then there would no longer be peak.

It is my sincere hope that you always want to improve yourself and your life. At the same time, counter the self-talk that tells you that your life is incomplete and that you need something in order to be happy. No, you want something. Why? Be honest about how it will improve your life and how you will, at the same time, be satisfied with your life in the absence of that thing. If you tolerate the discomfort of not having it, you may find that the discomfort subsides a bit. Is there really an urgency, or am I just creating one? Is my life as incomplete as I am making it seem? How is what I am telling myself helpful? The next thing you seek probably won't fill the gap.

Temper Tantrums While Driving

Road rage is a temper tantrum while driving. Face it—the world is filled with assholes. A fact of life in real-time. So why would you get jacked up because you encountered one while driving? Hell, if only one crosses your path in a day, you should be grateful.

Having an emotional meltdown while driving isn't about showing anything to the driver who pissed you off. It isn't about revenge or teaching a lesson. It is about you not controlling your emotions and going on to place yourself and others in danger because you are having a fit of frenzy. That is road rage.

When people tell me they, "can't help it," I see that as a giant cop-out. A person who can't help it is a person who does not have the ability to function safely in the world without supervision. Certainly, a person who cannot control emotional temper tantrums shouldn't be driving. I highly doubt this is what people mean when they say they, "can't help it." *I can't help* but think it means you don't have the ability to control yourself. That is useful as a general point of knowledge for those who interact with you, but I'm guessing that is not what you mean. It is also not something I would advertise.

I don't know why people give themselves permission to act out while driving, particularly at high speeds. The person who triggered you doesn't give a rat's ass that you were bothered by their rudeness, and going berserk to show the person how upset you are isn't particularly rational because the person doesn't care about that either. Trying to run the person off the road isn't going to teach the lesson you hope. That's a child's logic: A child begs for a toy, doesn't get it, throws a fit, and decides to teach the parent a lesson by holding his breath. "Watch me hurt myself to show you a thing or two!"

Set a boundary with yourself to reinforce that you are better than the person who baited you, and don't blame your own lack of emotional control on someone else making you do

it. That is also a lame excuse.

Fear: The Vine That Chokes

As humans, we are wired with a set of basic common emotions. We may not like feeling all of them, but I submit to you that we have these emotions for a reason. Your approval of said emotions is irrelevant.

While it may be confusing given what I just said, the emotions we have may or may not be rational given the situation or circumstances. For example, I might feel sad but not know why I am feeling sad. On a child's birthday, I may feel joyous and sad all at once—grateful for the moment and melancholy that moment passes too quickly.

I view emotions as data points that need context for interpretation. We need to identify what we feel and question what that means for us in a given time and set of circumstances. We get into trouble when we impulsively react to feelings as if their meanings are inherent.

Fear is an emotion that is particularly troublesome these days simply because there is so much going on in the world to feed the feeling. News headlines are filled with fear. Fear sells. If the news can invoke fear, people will watch because they want to know more. Fear also produces. Politicians know we will become activated if we are fearful. Advertisers understand this same principle.

The purpose of fear is to kick ourselves into gear to self-protect when we feel threatened in some way. Fear is meant to activate behavior. At the same time, fear is subjective. Some people are more prone to feeling fear than others. We may feel afraid because something in our present environment triggers a residual response from the past. We may feel scared because we jump to conclusions or misperceive something that is happening. Again, it is so important to notice the feeling, label the feeling, and interpret the feeling in a broader context in order to extract meaning.

Some people are more prone to fear-based thinking because of anxiety disorders. Others were programmed to fear through childhood experiences or traumas. Still, others are simply distrusting due to history or genetics around hypervigilance.

The problem is that fear can easily take over our minds, and when we are acting upon fear, we are completely irrational. The more out of control we are, the more people react to us by keeping their distance or reacting negatively to us, thus reinforcing our sense of alienation from others. We look at other people strangely; we keep them at arms' length. Then, they react strangely to us, and there is a vicious cycle.

Think of fear as a vine that keeps growing and growing. It becomes more and more tangled, and your attention is like watering the vine, making it grow even faster. Eventually, the vined area takes up all the space and chokes off healthier parts of your mindset. Fear chokes perspective; it becomes a cancer in your mind, making it impossible to take in any other perspective. You become paranoid, always in search of the evidence to support your fear-based thoughts.

We live in a world where there are absolutely things that logically induce fear; the problem is that humans are reacting as if *everything* is an existential threat. Fear has become an epidemic in our world. We fear for our health, safety, values, and way of life; we fear economic terrorism, world events, and natural disasters. Where will it end? If we live in total distress, we become relegated to a small corner of life, at which point, one could ask if it is really living at all. Life is a place where we make compromises between what we want and what we are willing to risk.

If we are going to find a place of enjoyment, we have to come to terms with fear tolerance. Life is found in the space where we feel the risk is worth it. And, I might add, it is focusing on oneself instead of always looking over one's shoulder to see what others are doing. When we lose sight of our own lives due to fear of others, we lose our joy and freedom.

Cancer is defined as cell growth out of control. Fear out of control can become a cancer of your mind if you let it. The good news is that it is curable, but you have to fight it off with good boundaries. Shut off the news. Actively remind yourself of what you can control. Look for the actual evidence of risk. Make a decision about how you want to live your life. Do you want to keep white-knuckling it through life? How's that working for you?

Say, "No" to the Emotional Self

As a self-proclaimed boundaries expert, I still struggle with them—mostly around telling myself, "No." I'm pretty good at setting boundaries with other people, but when it comes to my emotional self, well, that part of me is a vicious little bitch.

It feels as if I am telling my emotional self, "No" hundreds of times a day. Because I am human like you and exist with other humans in pain, I tell my emotional self, "No," when I am trying to do too much for others. I tell my emotional self, "No," around overindulging, especially in regard to trash food, and let's be honest here: I don't win that battle enough. I tell my emotional self, "No," around worrying, particularly at 2 AM.

Underlying all of this naysaying is intentionality. I ask what about the situation is pushing me to act in ways I would prefer not to act, what within me is reacting and why, and what I want to do about it. I have to consider logistics. For example, 2 AM is not a time to worry. I will feel lousy after I overindulge. My time and resources are not unlimited. When I say no to one thing, I am saying yes to something else. Just because I am inclined to do something doesn't mean that I should. Just because I think something doesn't mean it is true.

The most difficult piece is that there will always be internal pushback. The *yes, but*. My emotional self is not a pushover. My habits and drives are as fierce as yours, which is why I have to be methodical and persistent. Emotions are intense, but when emotions drive us, we are necessarily out of control because emotions are not always rational. To be maximally effective, we have to detach from our emotions and work to see the larger picture.

I often tell people that when the head and heart align, you have clarity. When the head says one thing and the heart says another, always, ALWAYS listen to your head. Your heart tells you the worst-case scenario. It tells you horror stories. It also tells you the greatest fairytales of all time. If only x would happen or y would change, then *everything* would be perfect. The thing is, your heart is known to be a liar.

The heart needs solid, steel, foolproof boundaries, or you are vulnerable to giving away money, time, and energy with abandon. Think of your heart or emotional self as your inner child who so desperately wants to believe in the best, naïve, larger-than-life outcomes, and you hate to tell the kid, "No." Yet, how do kids who have never been told, "No" typically behave? I am sure you see the big picture here.

The adult part of you is the wise mind that steps in to kindly remind your emotional self of facts. Sometimes, you have to tell your emotional self, "No," in order to avoid stepping into the same problems you spent the last year cleaning up, after which you told yourself you said you would never go through *that* again.

All of this will feel incredibly hard, maybe even *heartless*, but in the light of day, you will thank your wise self. Just because I've told you this doesn't make it easy. Your emotional self will throw fits, cry, and threaten you. A self-compassion-based approach is about coming alongside your emotional self with calming strategies, like deep breathing, journaling, or exercising. It isn't just about saying, "No." It is about soothing your distress and refocusing on other things you can do.

Setting boundaries with your emotional self is perhaps the most important boundary you can set. No one knows your own BS better. Call it out. Make a new plan.

Self-Deprecation Is Abuse

Some of us act like we were socialized to believe it is rude to accept a compliment. If someone says they like our hair, we react with disbelief. How could it be? Our hair is a complete mess. If someone appreciates our outfit, we are sure to say, "This old thing? I found it on the sale rack years ago." It is as if we feel the need to deprecate what is being said because we are unworthy somehow.

To be real, it is kind of rude to downplay a compliment. Someone says something nice, and our comeback is that they have bad taste? Poor manners, if you ask me.

The appropriate response is, "Thank you." Full stop.

What does self-deprecation get us? We are devaluing ourselves. Why? Do we think it makes us appear humble? Are we trying to one down ourselves? Can we not accept the fact that maybe we impressed another person in some way?

We've got to get away from the idea that accepting a compliment or stepping fully into our value is arrogant. Next time you find yourself ready to say, "Oh well, it was nothing," just say, "Thank you," and smile. It will be hard, but you will find it gets easier and easier. When you refute a compliment, you are really invalidating the person giving it. How inconsiderate is that? And how good does it feel to put yourself down in an attempt to appear worthy? Get over it.

Speech Therapy for Saying, "No"

Ralph is such a people pleaser; he finds himself in the perpetual situation of doing shit he doesn't want to be doing. He told me he *can't* say, "No." I asked Ralph if he had a difficulty with speech or pronunciation. Ralph was confused, and so I explained that *can't* means inability. I needed clarification on whether he was describing a barrier to speech. In actuality, Ralph was talking about discomfort with saying no, so he felt unable to use it.

Okay, okay. I'm an asshole, but I am making a point. Just because you feel uncomfortable using a word doesn't make it a bad word.

Saying, "No" is a permission you give yourself in full recognition that resources are limited. The allowance is acknowledgment that you are in the best position to decide how to use your personal reserves and articulating, "No" is sometimes the best, most appropriate response.

There is no possible way to please everyone, so start with pleasing yourself, which is more than possible and, in fact, the most responsible thing to do. Anything else gives others way too much influence over you.

The word *no* is a complete sentence and completely acceptable parlance. For those who are uncomfortable or unfamiliar with *no*, it won't feel good to say it the first few times, but it gets easier. It will not be that one day you feel good about saying, "No." The behavior change comes first. The emotional self catches up later with practice.

I know that you are good at annunciating, "No" because you speak it to yourself all the time as you are, "Yes" to others. You are probably so used to saying it to yourself that you have lost awareness. I suggest that you take a day or two and just, "No" to everyone as an exposure therapy. You may enjoy it so much that you will want to add some color, like, "Hell no" or "Fuck no." Start small and aim big.

Who the Hell Are You? (The Pursuit of Perfection)

Let me clue you in that there is no perfection, so if you stop chasing it, I may have gifted you several hours back into your week. You are welcome.

The pursuit of perfection is likely fueled by genetics or genetics plus early life experience. You may have been born a perfectionist, or you may have been groomed to be one as a child. Either way, just because I told you that you shouldn't be one doesn't mean you can snap your fingers and make it so. What you can do is recognize that chasing perfection is a road to nowhere.

Perfection is not possible, and to be honest, I wouldn't even know what it was or how it would look in real life. For many people, it is the desire to never make a mistake, and I understand that wish. Mistakes feel terrible. There is guilt, embarrassment, shame, humiliation. There is self-judgment and the fear that others will also judge. There is feeling not good enough, not worthy enough. It's best to avoid all that if possible.

What makes it worse is the sense that everyone is watching and noticing. First, this is mistaken because everyone isn't watching your every move. They are worried about their own performance more than yours. Most humans also respect that mistakes are part of life. Those who are hyper-focused on critiquing you are doing so only to divert attention from their own issues. There's no sense in giving that more attention than necessary, anyway. Finally, no one mistake or behavior is a referendum on your worth. **Read that sentence again.** Maybe post it on your mirror.

The desire to not make a mistake isn't the issue. It is being able to accept that mistakes or imperfections will happen. Imperfection comes with the admission ticket to life. The attitude of avoiding mistakes is to entirely miss their benefit. Alongside mistakes comes the massive value of learning, and mistakes are how learning happens.

The pursuit of perfection is a mindset of cutting corners, as if a person can just skip the learning part and get to the end result. Nope. That is not going to happen. Underlying the drive to be perfect is the idea that if you are perfect, no one can criticize you. Again, I have news for you. Haters gonna hate. Besides, there is always room for criticism. There are no get-out-of-jail-free cards on that.

I had a professor who used to say, "Who the hell do you think you are?" when I would get all high and mighty. I often use that phrase to challenge my own self-talk. Who the hell do you think you are that you get to be perfect while the rest of us are out here acting foolish? Seriously.

Perfectionism is a cancer of the mind that you must fight with self-compassion. It is reminding yourself that you are on a path of growth with the rest of us, and you are right where you are supposed to be. Pull up a chair. It is okay. You are okay. Learning is good. Don't let shame impede the learning.

If I told you that you should spend each and every day—most of the day, in fact—fighting aging, you would probably think I was a quack. Although we may want to make healthy lifestyle choices in order to live our best lives, most would recognize that we can't stop the aging process. It is a fact of life.

When will we get to the same mindset around mistakes? Mistakes are a similar fact of life. It is the judgment around errors that is so destructive. As humans, we don't like errors because we associate them with personal failings. We may call ourselves idiots or stupid. We may feel shame or embarrassment. This is equivalent to calling ourselves idiots for growing old or terrible, awful humans for aging at all.

Mistakes are necessary and, indeed, essential for human growth and development. Mis-steps inform our knowledge base as much as or even more so than doing something perfectly. Intolerance of mistakes is the same thing as denying or wishing away healthy growth.

I get that being wrong doesn't feel good, and they may come alongside serious consequences. Intentionality always has a role—meaning, did you wish to make that mistake? Avoidability is arguable. A mistake may have been preventable if you had knowledge or experience beforehand. Sometimes, we think we should have had the knowledge. But we didn't, so that is a waste of time. Sometimes, feelings and past experiences get in the way.

This discussion could go on and on; mistakes can be analyzed in perpetuity. Even so, we can't escape the premise that they are baked in as part of life. Stop fighting the inevitable and save your energy for the growth spurts that are to come.

Self-Improvement

The self-improvement industry is a multi-billion-dollar market. If you are reading this book, you have contributed to this bottom line. What makes self-help so lucrative?

Come closer.

People convince you that there is something wrong with you or that you can be better. These days, it gets easier and easier because you get on social media and see everyone's curated lives, which you can't possibly compete with, and you think, "How can I make *my* life better?" Then, there are a host of speakers, authors, and scam artists ready to give you that golden nugget of advice that will change your life.

Want to lose weight? Just do this. Want to make your skin tight? Rub this on it. Want to look cool? Wear this. Underlying all of this is the message that we are not okay as we are and that self-improvement is quite simple.

This is the bait and switch because nothing worthwhile in life is easy.

Surely, it has crossed your mind that I am a part of the self-help industry, so am I excluding myself? Yes and no. Because I consider myself a scientist and clinician, I feel that my guidance is at least based on actual self-improvement science. I don't peddle easy answers. I admit change will be complex and hard, perhaps lasting a lifetime trying to be better in some deep way, such as being more socially and environmentally engaged, being empathetic and compassionate, and being a better parent/friend/lover.

At the same time, I also believe that even if you aren't working to make yourself into a better person, you are still good, lovable, and worthy. I don't care about how you look, what you wear, or how much money you have. I dislike the superficial self-help that peddles the mentality of easy fixes or cures. Nothing in life is easy, and most things that are quick aren't lasting. True growth comes from hard work, pain, and effort.

I have met countless individuals who have spent thousands on self-improvement conferences, webinars, groups, and products only to experience disappointment that the *revolutionary* approach was the same rubbish they'd heard before. Yet, they keep trying, which, on some level, is admirable, yet also disappointing in that they choose the same get-better-quick schemes.

It's funny. I heard about the South Beach Diet for the first time in the early 2000s. It is essentially a low-carb diet, but I was naïve. I was telling a friend about how cool I thought it was, and her mom said, "That's the same diet that was around when I was young." I looked at her like she was so out of touch. This was new shit. Turns out, I was the uninformed. Never eating carbs isn't a reliable long-term plan. The same shit is repackaged every few years to look shiny, but it's probably older than you.

When you are considering your next self-improvement venture, ask yourself if it is realistic and able to provide lasting satisfaction. Be honest with yourself about why you want it. If you feel judged by it, it's likely a manipulation strategy meant to pull you in. Never allow anyone, including me, to make you feel less than just the way you are.

There Are No Awards for Martyrs

It is rare that I hear people share stories in which they are approached by work colleagues, bosses, and general others who tell them to stop and take care of themselves. Sure, your mother probably says this to you, but most likely, others are too busy benefiting from your effort. Your kids aren't saying, "Dad, take a rest. Let us cook dinner tonight," or "Mom, you go sit down. I'll handle the laundry." Hell no—that is not happening.

If we wait for others to tell us to take care of ourselves, it'll be a perpetual minute; giving up our own happiness to serve others doesn't come with an award. Self-care is a little like hygiene. You've got to make time for it and stop seeing it as optional or dispensable. It is to the benefit of everyone in your orbit for you to have good hygiene and be in good working condition.

Some people think self-care is something that fits in if there is nothing more pressing, or they view it as self-indulgent. There is nothing further from the truth. Think of self-care as putting fuel in the gas tank so your vehicle can operate, especially before it gets to empty. No one thinks that is ludicrous, optional, or over the top. It is a necessary essential.

Self-care is reinvesting in your mind and body health with metaphorical fuel in your tank so you can function amid life's unavoidable shitshow. What is self-care, you ask? It is an incredibly broad term, including but not limited to: eating food and drinking fluids that give you healthy energy; going for maintenance medical care in addition to when you have symptoms; saying no and having self-protective boundaries around people and things that drain your energy or expose you to toxic content or vibes; relaxing, having fun, spending time on hobbies, and being with friends and family who bring you joy; taking time off work, going on vacations, and spending time in nature; and giving yourself what you need to recharge and feel your healthy best.

The next time you tell yourself that you don't have time to do something for yourself, call out that bullshit. You aren't making the time, and there will never be a convenient time. There are no awards for martyrdom, and the mind and body don't run on empty.

The Self-Blame Factor

The concept *locus of control* was introduced in the 1950s by Julian Rotter and refers to the beliefs a person has about who or what is responsible for things that happen in their lives. [2] The original categories of locus of control include internal, external, and chance.

Internal locus of control refers to the conviction that people have control over what happens in their lives. For example, Shirin believes that if she works hard, she will get a promotion. External locus of control refers to people's acceptance that external factors, outside of personal control, control their lives (e.g., a deity or other people). Marty trusts that his recovery from COVID-19 is dependent on intervention from God. A chance locus of control means that people believe events happen based on chance or fate. Telly thinks that she will never feel better no matter what she does, so she doesn't do anything.

The type of locus of control you believe in has a significant effect on your behavior. If you believe that chance controls your future, I expect that you give up rather easily and tell yourself there is no point in bothering: What will happen will happen. If you believe a higher power is involved, maybe you pray or engage in behaviors you think will be pleasing to the higher power. All this may lead you to believe I am suggesting internal locus of control is a superior belief, which is not necessarily true. Internal locus of control is good when you set a goal and know that your hard work will get you to achieve the goal because you know you are personally responsible. There may also be times when feeling like a higher power is involved will help you even more.

Things go astray, however, when you believe you have control and things do not go according to your plan. Maybe you set a goal of running a marathon and train hard; however, you twist your ankle just prior to the marathon.

Do you blame yourself and beat yourself up because you believe you caused the injury? What if you get cancer? Did you cause it or deserve it? Did you drink too much soda or eat too much sugar? People with an internal locus of control often embark on missions to lay personal blame when things go awry because they believe they are, in fact, to blame.

Those with high internal locus of control are often achievers, but they are also the hardest on themselves when things don't go according to plan. They take side trips to purgatory as they beat themselves up for not knowing better, planning better, or doing better, as if they are responsible for all factors.

People who have an external locus of control may similarly be troubled when they don't get the response they'd been praying for. What does *that* mean? Am I not worthy? And those who are high on chance are protected when random bad things happen, like catching a virus, but they are less protected when there are things they could be doing, like washing their hands and wearing a mask in a crowded space.

Healthy beliefs around locus of control are balanced, meaning you believe there are some things that you can actually influence. Some happen by chance, and some you can blame on external factors.

This gets back to asking yourself about your self-talk. It is important that you ask who or what gets the blame. Where are you assigning responsibility? Credit? Punishment? It is also about catching yourself when you say that you can't or that you have no control. Is that accurate or are there are some things that you can influence?

While we may have certain tendencies, it is important to be aware of and challenge them. In the absence of evidence otherwise, folks with anxiety tend to jump to the conclusion that they are the cause of someone else's discontent. It is automatic self-blame. Catch that. Challenge it. Next time you give yourself permission to engage in unhealthy behavior because you have no control over your health genes, push back on those thoughts. Are they really in your best interest?

To survive in this world, we all need a bit of chance locus of control because bad things happen for no reason at all, and no explanation will ever make that feel better. Why do kids get cancer? Why do people abuse?

Sometimes, there is no explanation in the world that will provide peace to the soul. That, too, is the cost associated with the ticket to life.

Worry Is Worshipping the Problem

There is no way to live life without some worry, but life becomes intolerable under the weight of out-of-control worry. If one were to ponder all the bad or scary things that might happen in the course of a day, we would all stop living. We would likely freeze up or perhaps lock ourselves away—not that it would change the prospect of something bad or scary happening. More likely, it would be just enough to convince ourselves that we lowered our risk levels.

Living life is finding a way to exist with some acceptance that bad things happen. Worry doesn't change the outcome; it simply deletes any potential pleasure or enjoyment.

Some people tell me that they mistakenly feel if they worry enough, something bad won't happen. Note that I said *feel* because these same people intellectually know that this idea is crap. One way to manage worry, paradoxically, is to have a worry time. Set aside ten minutes each day to worry, and when you find yourself worrying at other times, you simply remind yourself that it isn't worry time.

Worrying just makes you sick and perhaps more likely to act in irrational ways. Bad things happen in life because they are baked in. Good things will also happen. All we can do is be where we are, live a little, learn a little, and find the strength to go on in spite of it all.

How do you want to exist here on this Earth? Do you want to worship at the altar of fear and worry, where the guaranteed outcome is not sleeping, having an upset stomach and headaches, and being edgy all day? Or do you want to quietly acknowledge that bad things can happen, but you choose to enjoy that they are not happening right now? The choice is yours.

Hit the Pause Button When You're Offended

I'm going to attempt to thread a fine needle here. As I am out living life, I believe in making every attempt to be sensitive to the needs of other people because it is the right thing to do, and it is not asking too much. I won't always succeed. I'm human; I have implicit bias; and I don't know everything. I am not always at my best.

But... at the same time...

I feel it is getting way too easy to be offended—it's almost as if people are seeking to be insulted, particularly on social media. Don't get me wrong. There is a lot to be offended by in our world. There is outright, naked hatred, bigotry, and cruelty. I am not talking about that. I am talking about when people make ignorant (meaning uneducated, unsophisticated, or unaware) remarks and off-handed statements or talk out of turn without the intention of hurting another person or group of people. (The use of the word *ignorant* itself can be misinterpreted as an insult because people don't know it simply means lack of understanding.)

To be clear, I am not giving people a pass to be uninformed. I am suggesting that taking offense is not a particularly effective response. Save that for people who mean to be rude. When we are offended, we generally respond harshly. In the case of someone who is unaware, the harshness or judgment may very well get in the way of providing a teachable moment. There is no growth. Nothing changes.

Being offended has reached such a fever pitch it feels like a movement, as if a group of people are lying in wait to pounce on someone who makes an ignorant remark. It seems like some folks are looking to be offended so they can go on rants about how they are, once again, hurt or victimized. This, in turn, fuels other folks to attack them as snowflakes. The pot-stirring is beginning to feel intentional, which furthers political divisions whereby each side believes the other has gotten too radical. I worry that it is like a relationship gone awry, a cancer in our society. The people who don't want to be put in a box are putting others in boxes, and so it goes.

What seems to be missing is consideration of intention. Yes, there are groups of people who intentionally say and do hurtful, oppressive, abusive things. No, not everyone who says or does harmful things intends to be hurtful. Is it possible to stop and consider intention? If not, we are on a collision course because there will be no safe space to communicate any longer. Just ask young people these days. They are paralyzed by the thought of being thrown out, shunned, canceled. The vibe is toxic.

I am asking for folks to hit the pause button when they feel offended. Not everything that is said and done is deliberate. I worry that everything is being turned into some kind of sin to be labeled, and there again is no safe space. I say all of that completely aware of the concept of

White fragility, and this is not that. I am not conveying that White or any other people are too fragile to have difficult conversations. I am saying that no one wants to have a conversation initiated in a wave of accusatory anger without considering intention or where judgment has already been passed.

Whether or not you are offended is a choice. I am simply suggesting that choosing to walk back feelings of offense and check them out first is the rational thing to do. Even if someone says something rude, I would argue that it only works if you allow it to become a cancer in your mind. As Viktor Frankl said about the experience of being in a concentration camp, "Everything can be taken from a man but one thing: the last of the human freedoms—to choose one's attitude in any given set of circumstances, to choose one's own way."[3]

I'd say that being in a concentration camp merited being offended, yet Frankl is suggesting that this is allowing the offender to take over your mind.

Being offended will do nothing to change the situation. Take a moment and check out your perceptions before jumping to conclusions, labeling behaviors, or attacking someone's motives before fully understanding them. It may be a fabulous opportunity for everyone to grow, and you are better for it.

The Throne of Self-Judgment

Truly, there is no worse critic of your personal existence in the world than yourself. That is due in part to the way the brain is wired: We are all egocentric. What I mean by that is our brains are wired to be focused on the self. We spend most of our time considering ourselves, our perspectives, and our experiences. We worry way too much about what others are thinking of us, but this is the confusing part. Others are also self-focused. It's a human thing.

You can label egocentrism as bad, but it is human nature—like it or not. It just is.

Because we are engaged twenty-four-seven in self-evaluation, analysis, and pleasure-seeking, we have lots of self-feedback, most of it nasty. We go into painstaking detail about things we have done wrong. To sweeten the pot, we heap onto those decadent helpings of guilt and shame. The point of these exercises is to ensure that we don't make any of the same mistakes, although the more we beat ourselves up, the more likely we are to give up entirely.

We don't stop with the past. In an attempt to avoid future mistakes, we also remind ourselves how likely we are to fuck up in the future. We imagine how others will laugh at us and judge us, but that also never works.

The fact is that self-judgment is all based on emotional malarky. Why? Because we are biased in how we view ourselves, and the bias may not be accurate. We also know more about ourselves than anyone else. We know the sins of our mind, our weak spots, and pressure points. We would never say some of the things we say to ourselves to other people. Our self-judgment is often ugly, abusive, and fear-based–and outright off the rails.

Self-evaluation or reflection, on the other hand, has merit. Evaluation is a systematic evaluation of positives and negatives minus the shame of judgment. We can all benefit from considering ourselves—just not in a self-annihilating way.

I've been asked why humans give such kindness and compassion to others when we don't give any of that to ourselves. I reply it is because we aren't looking into our own eyes. If we were, we would see a living, breathing, feeling human who is in pain and in need of a friend. Who better to be a friend than oneself? Only you know what you've been through, survived, and weathered. Give yourself a break. Your story is badass, and if someone else were telling it, you'd be crying already. Life is too damned short to condemn yourself to a prison of misery based on self-judgment when the judge and jury have been biased all along.

Enough with the Guilt

If you are ever going to be emotionally healthy, you need to come to terms with the idea that guilt is often a mistaken emotion. While we may feel guilt, there may be no identifiable reason to feel guilty, assuming that you have not been acting like an asshole.

Where does the guilt come from? Here are a couple of ideas. Maybe you have an anxiety disorder or depression, and guilt is a primary symptom completely unrelated to what is happening. Or maybe others effectively used guilt early in life to control or manipulate you. You may then carry the feeling into other interactions as a kind of residue or brainwashing.

Liza grew up in a very traditional family. Her mom seemed like a superhero. She was a fabulous cook and juggled extensive volunteer work for their church, school activities, and community events—all while maintaining the well-oiled machine of home-life. It was much later in life that Liza began to see how much her upbringing influenced her suffocating sense of guilt.

Liza's family was devoutly religious, and she recalls hearing regular messages of guilt at church. Her mother used guilt to cajole Liza into activities she would rather not have engaged in, and if Liza complained, there was a full-on dramatic reaction from her mom.

Liza worked very hard in counseling to say, "no," but she suffered from extreme guilt. Even if others gave her space to set limits, she guilted herself into stomachaches and headaches because she didn't have a good enough excuse to say, "no." She also guilted herself into self-doubt about being a good enough mother, partner, and person. Her crushing guilt began to morph into a sense of shame over not measuring up to the person she *should* be.

While the story of Liza is an extreme example, I have seen many versions of this type of guilt among women. Sometimes anxiety disorders underlie guilt, but there is often a strong undercurrent of early emotional brainwashing. I don't believe that parents intend to brainwash their kids, but it is a low-hanging fruit and a highly effective tool—one meant to control. Sadly, the after-effects are long-lasting.

I propose that guilt may be an indicator that our gullible emotional self has been activated. It is the job of the wise, adult self to evaluate the situation to see if guilt is tied to actual misdeeds. If you have called your partner an ugly motherfucker, you probably should feel a little (or a lot) guilty for the abusive insult. The guilt signifies that you need to apologize. The key is intentionally evaluating what is going on rather than simply responding to the feeling of guilt because it could easily be the case that someone is manipulating you.

Guilt can cause you to behave in ways that are nonsensical because, as I mentioned before, feelings are not rational. They are data, but they may be mistaken data.

Objective interpretation of the data by your wise mind is required.

If you are guilting yourself, particularly about the past, that is self-sabotage. Why do I say this when you may have done some terrible things in the past? Indeed, it is incredibly important to reflect on the past and to learn from the past so mistakes are not repeated. The use of guilt, however, skews perspective with shame and self-judgment. The addition of guilt doesn't add to or enhance learning. The past is what it is. It cannot be re-done even if you lay on the guilt extra heavy. What guilt does do is increase the likelihood that you act in even more irrational ways—like people-pleasing and emotional eating—anything to shut off the tired message playing in your head.

Set a boundary with yourself. Enough with the self-guilt. Self-flagellation with guilt leaves a mark that can indeed scar, and scars interfere with new growth.

Cancer in the Mind

It is undeniable that bad things happen. This is the first tragedy. The second tragedy is when we let those bad things become a cancer in our minds. What I mean is that we ruminate about the bad things. We churn and churn and churn on them. We bemoan that they happen. We second-guess and gaslight ourselves. We feel sorry for ourselves. Then, we begin to worry that they will happen again. We question our future. We get caught up in a sort of paranoia about what will happen next. We may even make it worse than it is by creating storylines of devastation. Then, guilt, worry, and grief make the situation feel even more haywire. Feelings of being targeted, punished, persecuted. They all come into play and serve as fertilizer for the ever-growing cancer of the mind.

Let me tell you the Buddhist story of the second arrow. Imagine it is a beautiful, crisp fall day. You decide to take a walk, soak in the colorful leaves, and breathe in the fragrant air. While you are on this relaxing walk, you are struck by an arrow. It is sticking right through your shoulder, and it hurts like hell. You can't move your arm. This is a terrible tragedy! You are bleeding. You need help. This is the first (literal) arrow. The second arrow is metaphorical. It is what you begin to do with what is happening, commenting on and labeling it in a judgmental way. You tell yourself that your experience is unbearable. What if you lose the ability to move your arm? What if you bleed to death? What if you lose your job? Who did this awful thing? Bad things always happen to me. Come to think of it, I should never have taken this walk. It was too good to be true. My life sucks, and here is another royal example of that. The first arrow injured your shoulder. The second arrow is the arrow of self-created suffering that you are stabbing yourself with, making a bad situation feel even worse.

The second arrow is also known as a cancer of the mind because it takes hold and rapidly grows. We can't always prevent bad things from happening. What we can control is how much suffering we create and how long we want to drag it out. We can control how big we let the cancer grow versus eradicating it on the spot.

I get that what I am saying may seem overwhelming—almost impossible—but it isn't. It just takes practice and a shit ton of persistence. We have to catch the catastrophic thinking, argue it, distract ourselves, and find a new perspective by whatever means we have available—be it talking with friends, journaling, or reading self-help.

Untreated cancer will destroy you because it is cell growth out of control, feeding on healthy tissue. Cancer of the mind is very similar. In this circumstance, you have the cure. Tragedies are unpredictable. Suffering is optional.

Horror Stories We Tell Ourselves

Let's say that your friend, Sonya, found a lump in her breast, and she tells you about it. Do you tell her that you are sure it is cancer, you are sure it is terminal, and she should begin planning her funeral to make it easy on her family?

Another scenario. Your adult son tells you that he thinks his fiancé is cheating on him because she has been busy with a work project involving an attractive coworker. Do you tell him that surely she is cheating on him, that he needs to confront her immediately, and that this was a foreseeable outcome because he is a piece of shit who doesn't deserve happiness?

I'm hoping you are appalled by what I am describing, yet it isn't so farfetched. We regularly tell ourselves the most horrific, terrorizing stories—mostly having to do with our unworthiness and how bad things always happen to us. The thing is, we would never say those things to other people. Why? Because a) it is cruel and mean-spirited, and b) we don't know if any of it is true.

So, why do we say those things to ourselves? Somehow, we think we deserve to hear it, or we think it prepares us or makes us better. Well, those are all fallacies or lies. Those nasty things we say to ourselves don't motivate us at all. In fact, they make us feel more beaten down, more worthless, and less likely to improve our performance at all. We begin to feel hopeless.

The next time you find yourself eager to pick up the scourge so you can start self-flagellating, ask yourself if you would say any of that to a friend or someone you love. If not, why in the fuck would you say it to yourself, whom you should love equally as much?

Self-love is self-care. It isn't narcissistic or self-centered. When people say that, I counter with the question: Is feeding yourself selfish? Feeding yourself is self-care. C'mon. At the very least, play by the same rules.

Horror stories are meant to scare people into submission or for entertainment by the campfire. Horror stories make people irrational. Next time you are trying to give yourself a nightmare, try dressing up in costume.

Imposter No More

Imposter syndrome is incredibly common. It is when someone feels they will be found out or revealed as a fraud. Most typically, when someone uses this phrase, they are referring to a professional role, but many people tell me they feel they are imposters in life. Sometimes we feel vulnerable to the scrutiny of others and wonder if we are deserving in a given situation. Sometimes imposter syndrome is a more pervasive and global fear of others finding out that we aren't good enough in a role.

I have felt this acutely when I give a talk and even when my books come out, and I attribute this to being vulnerable. In today's world, where others feel entitled to provide scathing public critiques that feel more like personal attacks, I am sure imposter syndrome resonates with a lot of folks. Imposter syndrome is a feeling that is completely detached from external evidence.

People who feel like imposters in life grapple with fear of being exposed as not a good human or not lovable or not deserving of attention, friendship, kindness, or love. As a result, these folks have a hard time even taking a deep breath for fear of rupturing a fragile equilibrium.

Tara describes herself as an empath, meaning that she feels deeply about other people's struggles and emotions. It is as if she can actually feel what others are going through. Tara describes her empathy as both a gift and a curse. She likes the compassion aspect, but she often feels so engrossed in others' experiences that she loses any sense of her own self.

Tara has come to understand that she gives too much to others partially because of her empathy but also because she is deeply worried that others will find out that she isn't a good person. She describes a sensation of constantly being on edge about her own worthiness, as if it is something she has to prove through her care for others.

While she knows she is a skilled educator, she worries that she will discover she is actually failing the kids she instructs. She can't let go of the fear that people at church will hold her in disdain for her sinfulness and shun her. Although Tara has been in a loving marriage, she wonders if her husband will find someone better, someone who will be a better partner and mother.

Tara knows with her head that her feelings are over the top, but she hasn't been able to stop herself from working extra hard to prove her worth in hopes this will prevent her fears from coming true. Tara has an imposter syndrome for life. The judgment she expects from others is soul-crushing. There is an element of social anxiety, but it is more than that: It is a feeling of being utterly unworthy of belonging to humanity and a chronic fear of exposure and being kicked out.

To be honest, I am not 100 percent sure where this feeling comes from—whether it is some sort of genetic trait gone awry or if it is from early childhood. I wish I could tell you how to make it go away, but if you are a fully-formed adult reading this book, it will likely never fully subside. You can, however, see the feeling for what it is— mistaken. See it as static, as a bad signal, as wrong.

People who are true imposters—that is, playacting to be something they are not—are generally con artists. So, if you are not a con artist in the factual sense, you are not an imposter. Humans are flawed. Every single one of us. No one knows everything. No one has all the answers. No one gets it all right. Because we are all in the same boat, we all understand that about each other. Those who are not accepting or understanding are the real imposters.

Your job is to recognize the faulty wiring and self-talk that tells you that you don't belong. It's a bullshit mistaken message. Stop listening and create a new one.

Praise and Glory

Everyone likes a pat on the back. It feels authentically good to be seen and appreciated. Craving that feeling is undeniably human and healthy. It is when we become preoccupied and driven to seek praise from others that things get out of whack. Praise from others can become like a crack habit, leading to always looking for another fix. This gives others tremendous power over us, and don't think for a moment that they don't know it.

The insatiable desire to seek praise from others negates the value of giving yourself praise. What about your own opinion or pat on the back? Does that not have worth? If you can see value in it, then you recognize there is the ability to give it whenever you want. There is tremendous power in that. There is no political agenda or groveling. You can tell yourself that you did a great job right on the spot.

Whether it is a survival skill or practicing what I preach, I tell myself, at least weekly, that I am a great parent—at least by my own standards. I mess up. I wing it. I freak the fuck out. I honestly don't know any other way to be a parent, but I do know that I can't wait around for my kids to tell me how awesome or appreciated I am. More often, I get the opposite of that. There is no glory to be had there unless I want to be penniless and without rules. Yes, I have to give myself the recognition I seek and be content with the occasional crumbs that come from others.

I will add to all of this that no one really likes a glory hound anyway. This is the person who is sucking ass all of the time in order to get public praise and glory in front of others. Being glorified in front of others enhances the deliciousness of praise because everyone gets to see it, which somehow makes some people feel it is even more valuable. I find this gross and kind of sad.

The core problem is seeking validation from others leaves you dependent on factors you can't control and vulnerable to manipulation and misuse by others. In case you haven't heard it yet today, your worth is inherent, meaning you don't have to earn worth. You have it regardless. You can do amazing things that others value and appreciate, but when you aren't doing those fabulous things, you are no less worthy than when you are. Anybody who tells you otherwise is abusing or manipulating you.

All that Stuff

There have been a slew of shows, blogs, and books written on the relationship between having too much stuff and unhappiness or dissatisfaction in life. Let me be real about my bias here. I am a minimalist, which causes another set of problems entirely. I am the person who regularly gets rid of things only to find that I need them later.

Too much stuff creates a sense of clutter or being boxed in or weighed down. Compare the experience of inner-city life with loud noises, mixed pleasant and pungent smells, lots of people, tall buildings as far as one can see, lighted signs, cars, and on and on. I've lived in large cities, and there are absolutely things I enjoy.

In comparison, one of my favorite vacations is Yellowstone and Gardiner, Montana. I remember riding horses in the morning into a national park where mountains were in the distance. It was quiet, soothing, peaceful. No buildings. No cars. Only the sound of nature. Being in nature enables me to feel present and whole. I find that being in the city is often over-stimulating in ways I didn't notice until I was in an uncluttered space.

I recall when I first visited New York City. I was a graduate student, and I was with a group of school colleagues attending a national conference. I was so excited as I saw landmarks and tried new things. One evening, we were getting ready to go out to dinner, and my heart started racing out of nowhere. It was literally pounding in my chest. My colleagues felt my chest and agreed that something was wrong. They were worried and asked me to sit and relax for a moment. The episode passed in a few minutes. I now know it was a panic attack brought on by over-stimulation. My central nervous system was yelling at me that I'd reached sensory overload.

I think this is similar to what goes on when we have too much stuff or clutter in our environment. Our brains are aware that it is too much and don't know what to do with it all. We probably got the stuff by telling ourselves we had to have it. It would make us happy. It didn't. We may have told ourselves that it was a great deal, and then we didn't use it. We may have kept something out of obligation because someone gave it to us, or we didn't know what else to do with it. Some things we may even hang onto out of buyer's remorse, and it is a constant reminder. My favorite example of this is hanging onto clothes in the hopes that after ten years we will *one day* fit into them again, and each year that doesn't happen is a disappointment. While we may want to get rid of it, we don't know how, so shit piles up.

Stuff is clutter. Whether you are consciously aware or not, your brain is attending to and processing the cues around you. Free yourself of the prison you are creating. You will find that the freedom of letting go of things is quite liberating. Stuff creates an expectation that you have to maintain it and protect it from being stolen or damaged. It isn't just the stuff. It is what you have to do to manage the stuff. Before long, the stuff rules your life.

Negativity

Psychologists tend to think that optimism and pessimism are genetic, so if you are negative by nature, it isn't by choice. That being said, it also is not a permission slip to be a negative nelly.

A negative mindset causes a cascade of problems, from physical ailments (pain, headaches, gastric reflux) to missed opportunities and people generally not wanting to be around you. A negative mindset is like a filter that colors all experiences in an unhelpful light. While the filter generally sucks, it can be altered. You just have to work at it. You have to force yourself to see what you are missing—to do a second look with more positive expectations. This takes practice but is doable.

Take the concept of self-fulfilling prophecy. What you predict to happen may very well come true because you expect to be so. If you look for the negative, you will get the negative. If you look for the positive, you get the positive.

The key point here is that our mindsets have so much more influence over our lives than we think. We make things happen because our beliefs shape our behaviors. As I mentioned, having a pessimistic cognitive style might not be your fault, but genes do not have final determination over our lives. We have choice and personal control over how our genetics influence our lives. If I tell you that a negative mindset will lead to physical and mental distress, what do you have to lose by redirecting yourself to look on the bright side?

Tell yourself *she is full of shit*, but then ask, *What if she's not?*

Positivity

Here I go again, seemingly arguing the exact opposite of what I just argued for. So, you thought I was saying positivity is good, right? Maybe.

Too much of any one thing is never good. I have heard people in tragic circumstances tell themselves that they *shouldn't* feel bad because others have it worse. I have also worked with folks who are suffering and yet tell themselves they *should* be grateful that it isn't worse. This seems very judgy to me, and I'm suggesting some boundaries around toxic positivity.

Positivity is good overall, but too much is judgmental. Think of it this way: If I am always supposed to be happy and see the bright side, there is never any space to feel sad or blue when I am having a bad day or things go terribly wrong. Not everything happens for a reason, or if it does, that reason sometimes sucks. Hearing that everything happens for a reason is seriously disparaging. What about when a kid dies from cancer? Explain the reason to me so I get it and feel peaceful about it.

If you are a positive person, you are lucky, but that doesn't give you permission to go around telling others how to be in this world. Even if you are prone to always see the silver lining, it is healthy to feel bad some days or not appreciate some events in your life.

As I've mentioned, too much of any one trait is not a good thing. Just keep in mind that no one likes the person who goes around appraising others for their positivity. It is entirely okay and healthy to have a bad day, to feel sad, to have a pity party for yourself. Allow for it. You just don't want to be the last one to leave.

The Rearview Mirror

Depending on your past, looking back may bring the comfort of nostalgia or the horrific pain of trauma. Either way, persistently reviewing, otherwise known as ruminating on, your personal history is not food for the soul. It keeps you chained to what has already passed. In other words, you are living in another time while your present ticks away. You miss new opportunities, react based on things not currently happening, and are distracted by a bygone experience.

Tito and Dan used to have so much fun together. Then Dan started distancing, and they seemed to argue all of the time about stupid shit. Tito often wonders if Dan is cheating, but Tito isn't ready to break it off. Instead, Tito spends hours reviewing the good ole days. He thinks about all of the fun they had and places they've been. Tito reminds himself that they could be that good again. He tries to ignore and suppress what is happening now. He compares the present to the past and now feels so less than. Nothing changes. They keep fighting.

Sometimes people aren't happy with their lives, and as an escape, they look to past memories. They try to convince themselves that the now isn't happening as they might believe. It is just too painful to acknowledge. The problem is that the past has passed. It isn't the current reality, and until the current reality is acknowledged, nothing can be done to improve it.

Sylvie went through a bad time when she and Todd broke up. Todd cheated on Sylvie for months, and Sylvie was devastated to her core when she discovered what was happening. Sylvie spent a year alone, unsure if she ever wanted to date again, but she eventually got out there. She found several people who were a good fit. Her friends told her how lucky she was to find potential in the shitshow known as dating. Where Sylvie struggled was trust. She seemed to drive each potential suitor away as she asked meticulous questions about cheating histories and could not refrain from rehashing what Todd did to her. Sylvie was stuck in past hurt, and she was pushing away others by assuming they would hurt her too.

These examples highlight how the past may hold different experiences, but in either case, the past detracts from the present. Sometimes when we compare the present to the past, it just doesn't measure up. Other times, we compare the present to the past, and we worry excessively that the past will repeat itself. There are things to learn from the past for sure, but living there stunts future growth. During challenging times, it may feel safe or predictable to revert to past memories. There is nothing wrong with reminiscing; however, when we get stuck looking behind, we miss the joyful experiences along the road we are on.

No Need to Look into the Crystal Ball

Our brains are wired to look for problems. It is what keeps us alive. We can't help that, nor should we entirely want to. The issue is when we become like some kind of laser beam constantly scanning for something to go wrong.

At any given point, an endless number of things can happen that we didn't account for and cannot control. A preoccupation with what might happen is a complete waste of time and energy. We can drive ourselves a bit crazy with *what if* thinking.

In order to find any kind of peace in life, we need to establish a balance between pleasure and pain. Enjoy what is happening while accommodating the reality that each moment is fleeting. Be where you are while you are there, knowing that in the grand scheme of life you won't be there for long. This holds true for both pleasant and unpleasant experiences. Successful living is tolerating the highs and lows.

How long will the good times last? How long will the bad times last? I wish I could tell you that, with enough planning, you will get around every problem that arises. Planning helps, but due to natural disasters, pandemics, bad weather, freak accidents, and the myriad unforeseen circumstances of life, it is a fallacy to think planning is foolproof.

The crystal ball can show you only one reality at a time, yet multiple realities exist all at once. Be here. Be now. Enjoy this. It is all we really have after all.

How Awful

Awfulizing is when we tell ourselves really terrible stories, perhaps worst-case scenarios—particularly if you are someone like me—on the high end of the anxiety spectrum. Awfulizing is "what-if'ing" on steroids. It is when we tell ourselves about dreadful things that might happen because, at some level, we believe it is motivating. Awfulizing is like mental terrorism that we unleash on ourselves.

What does awfulizing do? It makes us act out of control with fear. It makes us behave irrationally. It prevents good sleep and urges us to eat junk food. Awfulizing preoccupies us with making multiple contingency plans to prevent the worst-case scenarios before they've happened or before we've determined they are likely to.

Think about what you are saying to yourself when you awfulize. Would you say those things to a friend? If you think your neck pain is cancer, would you tell a friend who had similar pain that she probably has cancer, too? Would you say that to a child?

Yes, the frightful things you are preoccupied with might happen. So might a thousand other things. Which one do you decide to prepare for? How does that thought help you to be more effective in life?

I am suggesting that you are being your own worst enemy here. My question is: How's that working for you?

You Are Enough

When your inner critic calls you, "not good enough, "never good enough," or "unworthy," you have an immediate choice. You can believe it, or you can choose not to believe it. I say this fully understanding how real it may seem and how hard it may be to distance from that thought. The fact remains that there is a decision point confronting you. Not every thought you have is true.

Simon was an older man who came to see me, stating that he needed help coping with a new reality. Everywhere he went, people were talking about him. He could see them whispering, and he knew they were talking about him. He didn't like it, but he also didn't feel threatened or in danger. His wife told him that it wasn't happening, but Simon insisted that he could see it at the grocery store, at the ball game, out to dinner. Simon went to his physician, who put him on a medication aimed to make this experience go away, but Simon wasn't sure how this would happen. The medication helped somewhat, but he felt he needed additional coping tools to tune it out.

I told Simon that his brain was playing tricks on him. Since he wasn't feeling threatened, I told him that I could help him adjust by arguing back with his thoughts and distracting himself. He initially asked if I would be open to exploring in more depth if people were really talking about him. I told him, "No," and he accepted my invitation to argue his thoughts and perceptions.

Similarly, Eilsa came to me saying that she had spent her life feeling inadequate. Her mom emotionally abused her without mercy—telling her that she would never amount to anything and that she was a "leeching piece of shit." Eilsa no longer needed her mom to tell her what a terrible human she was; Eilsa told herself multiple times a day.

Both Simon and Eilsa had irrational thoughts that they automatically believed, and these thoughts made them miserable. Neither I nor anyone else could force them to relinquish their choice to unquestionably believe these thoughts, which were seemingly validated by their observations in life. What I could do was ask them what they had to lose by choosing not to believe.

The thoughts that you have that are not good enough are your brain playing tricks on you. Maybe it is from past experience or genetics. You don't need to try to convince me that the thoughts are real because I already believe that all humans are good enough. Yes, all humans can improve, and I hope they do. I believe all humans are worthy of effort.

The boundary that needs to be set here is the recognition that these thought patterns are self-abuse, and although it will be hard, you can choose to shut them down by detaching, distracting, or arguing. Abusing yourself is a choice that leads to nothing positive. Judgment and belittling lead to heightened self-loathing, which leads to more self-defeating behaviors. The pattern is perpetuated by the not-good-enough mentality.

No single person should require permission to feel worthy.

That attribute came with your birth certificate and was never meant to be earned. Imagine looking at a baby and saying, "You have to do everything I say and show me how great you are before I grant you love and worth." Sound ridiculous? The same principle applies to you.

Set a boundary here and now. No more using yourself as a punching bag. Be the one person you can always count on to say, "You are more than enough—as is."

Don't Take the Bait

We've talked a lot about walking away from others' toxic behavior, but what happens when you are the doer— when you are the one spewing toxicity at yourself? Being your best has a lot to do with defining what your best is. What does being your best look like in terms of behavior? I'm guessing it has to do with engaging in activities that bring you joy, eating healthy food, exercising, limiting unhealthy interactions, and limiting substances. It absolutely is choosing to stop yourself from doing the things that you have done in the past that ended badly.

Self-defeating behavior is activity that we know will end in our undoing, behavior that we know isn't healthy. Self-defeating behavior runs the gamut, like trying to control others, not standing up for ourselves, putting others' needs above our own, and going back to patterns that are not in our own best interest.

Give yourself permission to do the opposite of what might be automatic. The first impulse that comes to mind is very often not the best option. Prevent yourself from doing what you have done before that didn't work. Give yourself permission to be reflective and planful and not engage when the bait is set. Sometimes the biggest enemy lies within, and in this case, that enemy knows all the weak spots.

In case you have not heard this before, not responding is a response, and sometimes it is the best and healthiest response of all.

No One Wants to Hear That

Next time you find yourself poised to give unsolicited advice, know this: People don't want to hear that shit. It is judgmental and insulting. When you jump to giving unsolicited advice, you are essentially telling other people that you don't think they can solve the problem on their own. They need you to point out the correct thing to do.

Think about how it feels when you are bitching about whatever you have going on in your life and someone cuts in to tell you how to fix it all. The slap across your face is metaphorical, but I am sure bitch face settles in (or you are thinking bitch-face thoughts). *Thanks for that. I don't recall asking, but I guess you felt the need.*

Not only should you limit giving advice to people who've asked, but you should also limit your interactions with people who give advice to you when you didn't ask.

Maxwell's twin sister only wants to help. She was born bossy, and Maxwell was mostly used to it, although it was still annoying. He wants to share his problems with her, but she is kind of an asshole about it. She says, "What you really need to do is..." or "Here's how you handle that." Maybe she is right, but he never wants to do what she said because it is so intrusive. Maxwell just wants someone to listen and empathize. Sometimes he does want her input, but it would be nice for her to wait until she was asked once in a while.

I told Maxwell to start conversations with his sister by saying, "I want to tell you about something, but I need you just to listen. I don't want advice." Stated this way, it gives the other person—who is often telling themself you want solutions—permission to relax. Here's the thing: They can't know what you want if you have never told them. What we think of as common sense may be common only to us.

If you are a giver of unsolicited advice, take a big step back and ask yourself how condescending you really want to be. If you are a receiver of unsolicited advice, ask yourself how inviting you really want to be. What boundary vibe do you intentionally want to put out there?

Helping and the Fuck Budget

Being helpful is a true virtue, but there is only so much time and energy. If you have a helpful nature, it can sometimes seem that everyone is in need of help. At some point, we may find ourselves feeling like a victim of everyone and everything that seems to want something from us.

The reality is that much of the world needs our time, energy, and assistance, but those are limited resources. Enter best-selling author Sarah Knight.[4] With true genius, Knight suggests the concept of a fuck budget. Write this down.

Each day we are allotted a certain number of fucks to give, and they will not be replenished (as there are only so many to give). In this scenario, you need to start thinking strategically about how you want to spend your fucks because if you spend them willy-nilly, you won't have any more to give when big shit comes into play. It may be only in retrospect that you realize you spent all of your fucks on shit that didn't really matter.

Sometimes, people are into helping because it counteracts the delusional thought that they are not good enough or are unworthy. Helping doesn't make these thoughts go permanently away; it is only a momentary respite from an unquenchable thirst. Other times, people get overinvolved in helping because they haven't learned to say, "No," or they're easily manipulated. There are all kinds of reasons for helping to get out of control.

The point I am trying to hammer home is the role of intentionality. Help because you want to help and because it matters to you. Don't wait until it's too late to realize that you've wasted your fucks and left yourself fuckless—all out of fucks to give.

Your Good Intentions

Yes, you are reading that right. I am telling you to put a boundary on your good intentions. How could that possibly be a good thing? Have you ever heard of the platinum rule? The platinum rule states: Treat others as they wish to be treated. (Note: not as you wish to be treated.) Sometimes your good intentions aren't received as such because the person didn't want what you were serving.

If you seek to help someone who doesn't want that sort of help, is this your problem or theirs?

Misty was diagnosed with lymphoma and was flooded with people who wanted to help. It is a wonderful thing to find oneself surrounded by goodwill. All the offers to assist were well-intended, but some of the support was just given without an offer. People brought food, and Misty felt awful that some of it went to waste because she couldn't use it all. She was overwhelmed with attention, and she longed for some quiet time to reflect on what was happening. Her friends tried to distract her with activities, and she was conflicted. When she tried to say no, they insisted that she didn't know how much she needed to get out. They had gone to such trouble. Misty felt guilty that she wasn't more grateful.

People also shared their personal and family experiences with cancer. Misty was appreciative of the information, but it was a lot to process. People commented on how good she looked and how well she was coping and told her they were confident she would be fine. Their intentions were good.

In difficult circumstances, there is no one right way to behave, and hopefully, people in our orbit assume our good intentions. At the same time, it is important to reign them in and investigate the receiving end before bestowing your blessings. It is so easy to get caught up in a desire to help. No judgment here. I am just suggesting a speed bump between your intention and the person at the other end. What does the actual person need? What would be truly helpful? Have you asked? While you may notice how good a person looks or how well they seem to be doing, do you need to comment on it out loud?

Here is the hard part to hear. Sometimes our good intentions are more about making ourselves feel good than they are about helping the other person feel better. Read that again. Boundaries on good intentions are about getting beyond your personal need to help and thinking it through before acting on it. Sometimes the most valuable intention is being quiet and just listening.

If you see people as independent, resilient, and respectable, there is no need to insert yourself unsolicited into their lives with advice. We live in a very diverse world, and this ensures our survival as a species. You are not expected to always understand others. You are not expected to love everything about them or approve of their choices. Yet, you can allow those differences to exist without feeling the need to insert yourself, your opinions, and your values onto someone else. You do you, and allow others the liberty of self-expression without feeling like you have to make it about yourself.

Bella's mother-in-law is controlling. She has an opinion on everything, which is fine, but she takes it a step further and shares her opinion with everyone. Even worse, her mother-in-law presents her opinion as a superior fact, as she judgmentally tells other people, particularly Bella, what to do. This is super annoying, but when it comes to child-rearing, Bella is completely over it. Her mother-in-law's advice is never-ending, unsolicited, and incredibly entitled. What's worse is that Bella's mother-in-law behaves as if she is doing other people a favor by sharing her wisdom.

If this is you, I'm guessing you feel a bit misunderstood. After all, you just want to help. I understand that, often, a high need for control is driven by anxiety. What I mean by this is that a person's anxiety can be reduced by coming up with a solution, even if it is ill-advised. There is perceived closure. At the same time, other people don't want to hear your advice unless they ask for it. When you give it so freely, it makes others feel that you've encroached, uninvited, into personal space.

If this is someone you know, find your voice. You don't have to say, "Shut the fuck up" (although it is an option). You can just as easily say, "I'm feeling a bit overwhelmed with all of this information, and I don't want to talk about it," or "I appreciate the sentiment, but I've got this covered," or "Let's talk about something else." There are myriad ways to shut it down, but allowing someone to go on and on in an unwelcome way is almost like giving them permission to keep going.

Quick rule to live by: Don't insert yourself until you are invited. In so many ways, this is a violation.

Trips to Fantasy Land

Our brains are wondrous. They do so many amazing things. For starters, they run everything all at once. I can drive and problem-solve conflicts all at once. I can have a gut intuition that tells me something is off before the shit hits the fan. I can create an imaginary escape all in my mind. Imagination is just the best!

The trouble lies in fantasizing a bit too much. Nothing in the real world even compares to fantasy land, and that can be a downer. Fantasy land makes everything in the real world seem not good enough or wrong. It is easy to become unhappy with reality.

One really cool trick is when we go back over the past with a fantasy-land filter. We re-brand past shitstorm relationships as amazing. We were just too [stupid, lazy, distracted] to notice how great things were. Another fabulous tool is using fantasy-land Photoshop to look into the future. We are all living the *it* life with the *it* job and the *it* relationship, but there is no identifiable path to get there. No worries! In fantasy land, you just have to want *it* badly enough. If you doubt the possibilities, jump on YouTube or Instagram to see real-world evidence that you can be and have all of the wonderful fantasy land things you want.

I'm calling horseshit here.

Fantasy land is just that—fantasy, which doesn't mean a person shouldn't dream or want more. It just means that there has to be an element of realism, or life will be a series of disappointments. I don't know about you, but I think real life is so much more interesting, colorful, and exciting. Fantasy land only looks good, but I'm guessing you would get super bored there.

Sometimes I think I need bad days or moments to help me better appreciate good or peaceful moments. At least, that is what I tell myself, but I don't think it is simple comfort. If every day were amazing, how would we know because every day is the same? Get my point? Just like the pity party, visit fantasy land. Just don't stay there, or you

will find that the real good stuff has passed you by.

BOUNDARIES WITH PAIN

AROUND THOSE WE LOVE

(OR LIKE A LOT)

That's Not Okay

Hear me clearly. No one—not a single person out there—deserves to be abused by self or others. This begs the question of what abuse is. Abuse is misusing, being violent or cruel with the intention of causing harm. Abuse takes many forms, including physical and verbal modalities.

When you consider emotional abuse, which is typically verbal but can also mean withholding physical affection, the intention and patterns are crucial. I think, if we're honest, we've all had times when we said mean-spirited things or acted in exclusive, selfish ways. Abuse refers to having the intention to harm another person and often signifies patterns of behavior.

The challenge, for many people, is recognizing that abuse is taking place. It isn't always easy to see when you are smack in the middle of it—no matter how smart or informed you think you are. Sometimes abusive behavior is all a person has known from family and others early in life.

Perhaps the trick is asking yourself how you feel around someone. Feeling afraid, feeling you are walking on eggshells, feeling belittled or shamed or frozen out—these are all associated with abuse. Sometimes the best way to identify abuse is to identify how you are feeling about the way another person treats you.

The boundary here is making the commitment right now to not allow abuse in your life. I recognize that it may not be as easy as it sounds. When people are in abusive relationships, it is life-changing to leave. Child custody, finances, and safety are all issues. I never tell someone in an abusive relationship to just "Leave!" Leaving abusive relationships significantly increases the chances of mortality.

What I am saying is to make a personal commitment to yourself not to tolerate abuse. I am asking you to acknowledge the reality that no one deserves abuse and to grant permission to get help if you are experiencing abuse. If you are not in an abusive relationship but find yourself in an abusive circumstance, be it at work or otherwise, you will know this is not okay. Indeed, even if it is your mother, sister, or brother who is the abuser, it is not okay.

This is a basic foundational level commitment that you owe to yourself: Make a plan and ask for help. Call 1-800-799-7233, go to thehotline.org, or text START to 88788.

The Knife in the Back

Megan, Tess, Berta, Maude, Phyllis, and Diedre were besties. They were in constant contact via group texts. They hit all the summer concerts and had their own silly celebrations. The group was rock solid and had the kind of adult friendships they wished they'd had as teens: authentic and unquestionably supportive. They were closer than most families.

Until they weren't.

One day, Phyllis had a tense exchange with Tess and afterward vented about her to a coworker. She shared something about Tess that was private, and Tess found out. Tess was devastated and confronted Phyllis, who became defensive and blamed Tess for the whole situation. The two had it out and said some pretty terrible things, using intimate, personal information to strike deep emotional blows. They walked away, swearing to be *done*.

Megan, Berta, Maude, and Diedre were dumbfounded and didn't know what to do. A lot of side texting started. Megan found out that Berta and Maude had lunch with Tess. She called Diedre, who was pissed. Phyllis was trying to cull the others to her side and suggested that they choose her as a sign of loyalty. The once inseparable group was in shambles.

All of this happened three years earlier, and Tess was still living as if it had happened yesterday. She was incapacitated with anger, grief, and hurt. She still couldn't believe Phyllis had stabbed her in the back by betraying her confidence and then blamed her for the way it went down. Tess felt that her friend group had abandoned her by not taking her side, and she stalked Phyllis and the gang on social media. When she discovered they were all at a party together, she was infuriated, as if the betrayal were happening all over again. She was miserable and felt numb much of the time. She just couldn't break out of the disloyalty and heartbreak.

I see folks all the time who have trust issues over infidelity with an adult friend, and that sense of being stabbed in the back is magnified by ripple effects within the social circle. These fractures of trust have a deep impact on one's sense of self and safety. What it stirs up, I believe, is all of that self-doubt and insecurity of adolescence, when we wonder what is wrong with us and when friends are so central to our identity and sense of security in the world. It feels like a referendum on our worth.

If we are to heal, we somehow have to find a way to trust while co-existing with the reality that we might be hurt by another. If we are not able to repair that situation, we have to find a way to move on. I don't usually call this forgiveness because people get too caught up in concern over whether or not forgiveness is deserved. Instead, I call it finding peace.

Finding peace is not saying you are over it or forgetting about it. Instead, it is trying to transcend the toxicity and negativity so that you can go on with life. It is rising above the drama of trying to get people to choose sides, to choose us—because it is not a contest. It is not a competition for attention. The desperation of trying to control the narrative and trying to coerce others to side with us doesn't fill that empty, insecure space inside.

When someone betrays your trust or hurts you deeply, that is on them. Stop making it more about you than it needs to be. Give yourself the healing you seek. Provide for yourself the love and kindness your soul desires. Stop putting yourself out there for others to choose or reject.

While it hurts deeply, the healing you seek is something you can provide for yourself. Remove the knife, heal the wound, and stop looking for others to give you temporary relief. What you wish for is within your grasp.

Parents Give, Kids Take—Rinse, Pause, Repeat?

You can't blame kids for taking all that we are willing to give. That is their job. It would be seriously foolish to turn down the perks of having your heart's desire fulfilled by others. Take some perspective here.

The cycle of parents endlessly giving without thought can create a codependent, leeching cycle that leaves parents feeling resentful and kids feeling incapable of doing for themselves. The parent's job is to teach kids about limits and boundaries, which necessarily means saying, "No."

Remember when I talked about healthy development? When I said our job as parents is to teach kids to be independent? That involves learning the meaning of the word *no*. No is healthy. It is life-affirming. It is life-sustaining. We cannot, however, look to our children to validate such limit-setting. They don't want to hear "No." It isn't in their short-sighted interest. It isn't enjoyable, and it isn't exciting. As parents, we have to know the value of saying no without getting our kids' approval.

Step to the side and think about what I am saying because I see it all the time. We, as parents, sometimes find ourselves second-guessing our decisions because our kids don't like them. This is the very tough job of being a leader. We have the big picture in mind, and we cannot expect that the vision will be shared by folks who don't have all the data we have.

I understand the pressure of wanting to be liked and appreciated by our kids, and it can feel so good to do things that make them happy. When we do this too much, however, we don't teach them the meaning of boundaries. We may tell ourselves that we are making them happy when we are actually making ourselves happy by choosing the low-hanging fruit. The harder and more important lesson for them is to cope with not getting their way. Life is full of disappointments.

Reframe: Childhood is the perfect time to learn to manage distress and how to bounce back. Just by saying no, you are providing your kids with valuable skill-building opportunities. Read that again. Rinse. Repeat.

Enabling Only Works with the Unable

This take very much relates to the previous take. Codependence is a desire to help that has gone out of control—meaning the codependent person does not know when to stop helping. As a result, the person you are helping begins to depend on your so-called support, and it is an unhealthy attachment.

Let me give you some everyday examples because I think a lot of us find ourselves in these situations.

Mechelle has a teen who struggles in high school, particularly around turning in homework. Mechelle wants her teen to succeed, so she asks her daily about homework, follows through to make sure the homework is in the backpack, texts her to turn in the homework, and emails the teacher to see if it is done. There is good intention here, right? Well, one day, Mechelle forgets, and the teen blames Mechelle for not reminding her. The teen has come to need Mechelle in order to get work done. Codependency has cemented. Mechelle's behaviors serve a need, and her intentions are good. The problem is that her daughter is not growing in abilities. How will her daughter learn to do the work on her own when she goes to college? Mechelle tells herself that she can't let her daughter fail because the consequences are too high. In her mind, it will eventually work itself out, except that it doesn't.

Garth has a son, Ben, who was bullied mercilessly at school via social media. Garth took Ben to counseling and worked with the school, but Ben continued to struggle with self-esteem. Ben got through college with a bachelor's degree in sociology, but he has not been able to find a job that pays a decent wage. He moved back home with Garth and is depressed. Garth feels sorry for Ben and is giving him space to sort out his life. Ben lives rent-free, isn't working, and isn't really looking for a job. Ben sleeps until noon and hangs out with friends. Garth is happy that Ben is spending time with new friends as it is good for his spirits, and at least he isn't using drugs. Garth worries if Ben will ever become independent, but he buckles under the guilt of feeling responsible for not protecting him.

Milt and Arman were super close growing up as brothers, but Milt was the oldest. He recognized that his parents favored him, even though he also knew this wasn't fair. Arman wasn't as tall or athletic, as social, or as achievement-oriented as Milt, but Arman had other talents. He was exceptionally kind, compassionate, and creative, and he was always willing to help others. Milt built an incredibly successful life, and he always felt badly that Arman was less financially successful. Milt felt guilt that he was somehow responsible for Arman not achieving more because of the way his parents differentiated between them. As a result, Milt was very generous with Arman. Arman had a lot of business investment ideas, and Milt was there to fund Arman. Milt didn't want to crush Arman by saying no, even if he felt the venture was ill-fated. Milt started to feel resentful that Arman relied so heavily upon him, but he then guilted himself into continuing the pattern. Arman was grateful, but he also felt that Milt had the money to give. Arman was ashamed but eager to prove himself again and again.

Each of these scenarios highlights codependence. It typically involves a significant investment in someone you love and could not possibly imagine turning your back on. Feelings of guilt drive behaviors, and the end result is an unhealthy symbiotic relationship. The person who is receiving care is prevented from growing, and the person giving the care is prevented from learning to manage anxiety, guilt, fear, and perceived loss of control.

Because codependence often initiates from a place of love and concern, everyone has the potential to find themselves in a codependent relationship. It quickly morphs into control and dependence, power and hierarchy, and developmental arrest.

Regardless of the positive intention, codependence is not healthy because it is a burden for all involved. One person is carrying the heavy load of feeling responsible for another person's choices. The other person carries the weight of stagnating.

When you find yourself feeling a bit codependent, remind yourself that doing too much actually prevents another person from growing. Challenge yourself to tolerate the deep pain of watching another person experience growth. The suffering you create by telling yourself horror stories is optional.

Family Drama Is Baked In

Just because you've read about boundaries and generally agree with their importance, it doesn't make it any easier to practice them. There are no people in our lives more difficult to set boundaries with than family of origin. I am talking about the people who raised you. These are people who had an influence on you before you even knew what influence was. They are people you are attached to, people you love (or hate/love), or people you are confused about. These are the people who piss you off like no other. They make you feel gaslit, loved like no other, inadequate, and essential all in one conversation.

Family knows you inside and out. They know your weaknesses, blind spots, and vulnerabilities. We have history with family. We have stable, predictable patterns of interaction, and these are incredibly hard to break. The guilt I referenced earlier is never stronger than when setting boundaries with family, yet boundary-setting is necessary.

Your family is no more likely than anyone else to know what you want and need unless you tell them in ways that they understand, and this may mean telling them over and over and over. Other times you have to show them with action, like ending conversations, walking away, or not responding at all. There are even times that family tests you to be sure you mean it. It is common for family to feel they know more about what you need than you know what you need. Boundaries, here, are about establishing a new way of being with family to ensure that your wants and needs are represented—not more important than others' needs but at least on equal footing. Then, you get to decide what to do next. If you are practicing the principles of respect and communication we have discussed, then guilt is the only residue to be washed away.

That is not to say that setting boundaries with family won't be fraught with emotional landmines. Others will know your buttons, and they will push them to get you to back down. They know your weak points and will use them against you, not to hurt you but to get what they want. I say all of this so you are prepared for what is to come when setting boundaries with family. Remind yourself that the goal is to improve your relationships, and this will require fortitude and courage. It is incredibly hard and often painful to unravel all of the emotional baggage that comes with family relationships and shared history.

What's the payoff? The long view is that it is better to have authentic, pleasant interactions with family than to play-act and be resentful. Where will being dishonest get you anyway? (Hint: trouble and repeated fights about the same issues.)

Ready for a change? If it is going to happen, you will have to own the effort. They can't read your mind, after all.

Yes, Love Has a Boundary, Too

You may think this is complete heresy, but yes, I am suggesting boundaries around love. I am not suggesting that you can control how you feel, but I am proposing that you put your head in the game of love alongside your heart. While your emotional self is fluttering around in the land of fantasy and perfection, firmly plant your wide mind in the watch tower of reality. Be on alert for red flags—when your heart says, "Maybe I'm being too picky," "I'm sure I'm overreacting," "He always has a good reason," or "I am sure it won't happen again."

Some people believe that you shouldn't have to think when you're in love. It just all falls into place. I'm here to ruin all the fun when I remind you that the moment you let your head check out, the whole operation is at risk.

When Tasha and Charmaine met, it was like electricity. The physical connection was undeniable, and this only fanned the flames of interest. They quickly became inseparable. Each found the other so different from anyone they'd dated previously. It was as if they were discovering parts of themselves that they didn't know existed. Tasha would tell you that they were completely different and that Charmaine had none of the qualities she thought she wanted. Tasha is a planner; Charmaine is completely spontaneous. Tasha is a liberal to the core, while Charmaine is on the conservative side. Tasha is introverted; Charmaine is extroverted. The differences between the two were wide and lengthy, but there was no ignoring the chemistry of opposites. Tasha threw her mate wish list out the window because something that felt this good couldn't be wrong. They moved in together, and things went to shit almost immediately. They started fighting like cats and dogs over everything from how to do laundry to what news channel to watch.

What am I saying here? That you shouldn't follow your heart? Nah. That's not it at all. I am saying that with regard to relationships, it is important to put your heart or emotional self in the passenger seat and give the steering wheel to wise mind.

In Tasha and Charmaine's case, I wouldn't advise shucking a good thing. By all means, enjoy! The missing piece, though, is having a reality check in place. The feel-goods associated with blind love won't last forever. Caution dictates going slow, being watchful, planning for conflict, and having a plan for managing the unpleasantness of being in human relationships.

Love alone will steer you to the most beautiful places. But without GPS navigation or road maps, you may find that you've overshot your intended destination. A boundary on love is a wise-mind reminder, like a parent raining on your parade by telling you not to do that thing that sounded so cool in the moment. You later realized that your parent was brilliant.

Fido Knows Exactly What He's Doing

Truth time. This is also a problem for me. There is something about looking into the eyes of our beloved pets that challenges even the strongest of resolves. What is perhaps even more troubling is how I know that I am projecting my own thoughts and feelings onto my pet even while I am doing so, but *those eyes*! They just look so innocent, so forlorn. I start telling myself stories of how Bacon (my dog) is feeling and what he is feeling, and I want to give in even if I know that giving in is the last thing I *should* do.

Time to cut the crap with the pets. I implore you (and myself) to stop making eye contact when you feel weak. For the love of life, look the other way. Another cookie is the last thing the dog needs, and the cat is using you. Indeed, the cat may be smarter than all of us. This you know.

Just as your inner child needs tough love sometimes, so does your pet. No advice is gonna make this easier. Avert your eyes to avoid hypnotic gazes. Steel your nerves. Tough love, my friend. Tough love.

You Do You

It's tempting to become preoccupied with the faults of others. Let's be real. There is a lot to distract us. Yet, when the finger is always pointed outward, much is being missed in our own self-improvement. It's easy to focus on what others are doing wrong and what they can do better. It's not so easy or so entertaining to focus on what we can do better. The finger pointed inward is a direct challenge to safety, status quo, and moral superiority.

These days, we live in a society where it is starting to feel normal to openly judge others. We judge people's appearance, life choices, and behaviors—all without even knowing them or their stories. It is a comfortable place to sit—in judgment of things we have no clue about. I see it as a means of control. How in the fresh hell can we know what is the best choice for another person without having walked in their shoes? Or they in ours?

I cannot tell you the number of new, young mothers who have come to see me with postpartum depression, sharing the burden of feeling substandard. They have been told the rules for being a good mother, which felt oppressively high even before having baby. Consider breastfeeding. In order to be a good mother, healthcare providers and society at large tell mothers they must breastfeed. I mean, what kind of mother would not want her baby to have the best available nutrition and protection from infection? When breastfeeding doesn't come easy, these new mothers report being shamed for doubting and being pushed to physical limits when they are completely exhausted. They are discouraged from considering bottle feeding because it is a sign of failure. Who wants to be a failed mother?

Excuse me for objecting to this tyrannical dictation of what is right for baby without simultaneously considering what is right for mommy. If mommy isn't okay, baby likely isn't going to be okay. Not every mom and baby has to breastfeed, and scaring new moms into thinking that they are damaging their babies if they don't is cruel and wrong.

Society does this. We create these rules, apply them as if there is a one-size-fits-all, and use guilt as a primary manipulative tool. Child-rearing is just one example. We create simple plans for other people to revamp their lives without breaking a sweat. Easy peasy. When thinking about our own problems, it's not as simple or clear-cut. There are reasons we engage in nonsense. We have issues, extenuating circumstances, and relationship considerations, and it's hard to change. There are ripple effects. Well, fuck all of that.

I get the allure. While we are busy making rules for other people, we are distracted from our own problems. And it is so very easy to do. Maybe it is also a bit satisfying because it allows us to feel better about our own lives and choices. I mean, at least we aren't doing *that*. Interestingly, some of the people who gripe the loudest about rules are some of the first to engage in making new ones for other people.

Regardless of how much others need to do better, you can't control that (besides it being none of your business). You can control only your part, and to be clear, that is more than enough. The distraction element is real and seriously judgmental without all the facts. Seriously, your shit smells just as bad, if not worse.

I beg you to resist this trend. At any given moment, people have struggles we know nothing about. There are backstories that we haven't read. There are histories we haven't experienced. There is no authentic satisfaction to be had, elevating yourself in comparison to another person through judgment. It is not your job to police other people.

At the same time, I understand that social justice issues threaten whole groups of people. I am not talking about that. I am talking about individual lifestyle decisions. It is not okay to impose your will or beliefs upon other people. Even when you try, it doesn't work because it causes people to become more entrenched in the opposite.

If you find yourself surrounded by people who judge, it is time to look for new soil to plant yourself in. All of the judgment takes a toll. It is insulting. You will never be enough, and you will never feel safe being yourself. Folks who judge you do so under the guise of just trying to help or just trying to make your life better. I call horseshit on this. They may tell themselves that is the reason, but it is not. It is more about control, self-elevation, and distraction from one's own set of issues. Take a step back. The burden of judgment may be choking off your life.

We have already discussed that time is the most precious and probably the most squandered resource. We have already discussed inserting yourself where you haven't been invited. You don't have time to police other people.

Hear me clearly. I am not saying that we should not care about health and welfare and social justice issues. I am saying that we will not get anywhere by policing other people as individuals in a free society. I don't want anyone shoving their values down my throat, and as a result, I don't feel super thrilled about trying to shove mine down someone else's. I embrace the philosophy, "You do you, and let me do me."

Let's make a deal. For every time you point the finger outwardly, point it back at yourself and ask what you can do better (minus the harshness).

A Special Kind of Pain: Teenagers

I'm self-aware enough to know I may be writing this because of my own issues, but I also have a lot of folks who consult me about their concerns with parenting teenagers. It's a real thing—a really painful thing.

Being a teen these days seems exceptionally rough. Beyond all of the hormones and emotional angst of feeling insecure and inadequate, there is the inescapable effect of social media to put everything on display for commentary. There are also school shootings, climate change concerns, and a general pessimism about economic independence.

That is the teen side. Then, there are the adults who love these young people and watch them suffer. Being a parent of a teen is like investing all your money into an account and never having any valid evidence if you are making or losing money and accepting that you will not know for years to come. The worry is soul-crushing.

A parent's natural tendency is to want to intervene and fix all the teen's problems, which often leads to intense, volatile arguments. A parent trying to give guidance to a struggling teen can feel like someone trying to pet a hive of angry hornets.

No one comes out of this satisfied or relieved. Teens feel misunderstood and judged. Parents feel rejected and disrespected. This boundary is written for parents.

Do not despair. Pay attention to the fatalistic story you are telling yourself. It is causing you to escalate the anxiety. Adolescence has always been and continues to be turbulent. The goal is that the teenagers are trying to figure out who they are and who they want to be separate from you. How can that not be painful, especially in this day and age?

Here is some important food for thought. Americans deeply value independence. Therefore, traditional models of human development within US culture strongly emphasize differentiation compared to other cultures. What I mean by this is that as we raise our children, our goal is to cultivate independence so that our children can survive without us. We want them to be strong and self-supporting as a means of survival. There is less emphasis on keeping them at home within the family of origin. If you want your teen to be independent, you need to provide a safe space to experiment with that, including a safe space to fail. You have the opportunity to teach your kids boundaries that perhaps you didn't learn.

If you subscribe to the idea of nurturing children to be self-supporting and independent, you can appreciate the importance of boundaries as central to healthy differentiation. Boundaries are all about establishing oneself as individual and separate from family, friends, and important others. This is not an insult to family. It is simply a declaration of autonomy. This is why I tell parents to support (or at least tolerate) adolescents and young adults

as they push back or talk back. It is theoretically healthy.
Teens are exploring who they are as separate from their
parents. Usually, it is not threatening unless we choose to
make it threatening. (Of course, I am not talking about
violent behavior or grossly self-harmful behavior.) Pushing
back is part and parcel of the exploration process that helps
young people discover individuality in this complex world.

Having said all of that, the experience of young
people breaking away can be incredibly scary for parents.
There are a lot of unknowns. We want to protect our kids
and save them from our mistakes. The problem is that there
is no way for young adults to learn about life without
making some of the same mistakes. It is all necessary in the
developmental course, and as I mentioned previously, there
are great lessons about boundaries along the way.

Parents, stop telling yourself horror stories. Stop
taking everything they say literally. They don't hate you.
They want you to back off, but not all the way off. They

push to see if you will stick around. Be a calm presence.

Show them unconditional love. Believe in them. Celebrate

the wins, and definitely have a self-care plan. Exercise.

Talk to others who listen and don't judge. Take breaks. It

really is a marathon rather than a sprint, and parenting is,

quite literally, the hardest job I've ever had.

BOUNDARIES WITH PAIN

AROUND SOCIAL LIFE AND

WORK

Healthy Competition or Rivalry?

Social comparison is normal and, in some circumstances, can even be healthy. For example, when you get bad news and compare yourself to someone who has it worse, you might feel grateful that it isn't *that* bad. But problems arise when there is a competitive comparison with others that leaves you feeling not good enough or less than. As a result of this feeling, you try to outdo or outshine others for the wrong reason. You aren't doing it because it is something you want to do; you are doing it to compete with someone else.

Anthony and Joseph both worked in sales. Their partners and friends hated when they all got together because it quickly became a brag fest. Each tried to outdo the other in sharing commission data. Each proposed to know more about the market than the other. On the face, it seemed like a friendly competition, but it was uncomfortable to be around.

Here is another scenario that might be familiar. Each year at Christmas, Bettie Jo and Christine vied for the attention of their parents. As sisters, they were always being compared by their family: who is taller, who has better grades, who is going to what college, and whose kids are better behaved. As adults, they've grown accustomed to winning praise from their parents, often at the cost of respect for one another. They went to great lengths to select the most original, expensive gifts, bring the tastiest dishes to share, and show off their respective families, who appear to have stepped out of a catalog photoshoot. Family gatherings took on a vibe of superficiality rather than true holiday spirit.

Competition for superiority can take on a life of its own. The competition may be social—who is throwing the best party, or who is invited to the most parties? It might be on social media—who has the most likes or appears to be having the most fun? It might be physical—who looks the best or is the most athletic? It could be at work—who gets the biggest bonus or has the most positive reviews? The possibilities are endless.

While I think some competition is healthy in sparking each of us to elevate our performance, it can easily lead to obsession, where it becomes more about having to be better in order to feel worthy or better than. It may be about wanting to show up another person to feel accomplished. Our self-worth must come from our own self-judgments. Otherwise, we are at the whim and under the control of others. If our own self-judgment is dependent upon what others are doing, we have given up our own internal compass, and true north will forever be dictated by others' activities, standards, and values.

If you find yourself surrounded by others who are competitive, maybe you need to set a boundary with them. True friends celebrate you for who you are and don't feel the need to one-up you. You may discover that it isn't friendship after all. Maybe it is a rivalry for glory.

How do you know the difference? Ask yourself how it feels. If it feels tense and not fun, it probably isn't for fun. I'm guessing if you dig deep, you will find your greatest adversary lives within you. Now, what do you do with that?

Attention Seeking

Attention-seeking people crave the spotlight. It is as if they need to be noticed in order to breathe. I find this annoying as hell, probably because I am completely opposite, which is surely irritating in a different way.

Misti seemingly couldn't help it. No matter where she went, she found herself the focus of attention. She dressed in ways that got people talking. If someone had a story, she had to tell a story that was wilder, funnier, and more whatever point was being made. Misti spoke very loudly. Her emotions were all over the place. She cried at unexpected times. No one could ignore her laugh, and she yelled a lot. And don't even get started on getting a man's attention. When a group went out, Misti did not stop until she had the most male attention in the situation. Misti would never be outdone, especially on social media. If Misti wasn't getting interest from others, it was like she didn't exist.

Attention from others will never be enough to fill the insatiable thirst that is really about filling a void inside. The void is temporarily filled, but more is quickly needed. It's a vicious cycle, and the hunger gets more and more overpowering, driving away others who are put off by it.

I would like to quip that a person who does this should recognize it and stop, and I wish it were that easy. I do think recognizing it is important, but afterward, asking for professional help is essential because the attention hunger doesn't go away. Therapy helps to find healthier ways to feed the hunger by doing things for oneself rather than always needing an external fix, like, or appreciative comment.

You may not have been told in your life that your worth is independent of notice from others, and perhaps you've been on a lifetime quest for that affirmation. Now is the time to control the mixed-up drive for attention and external validation. You are enough. Get some help seeing that for yourself.

Oversharing

Cedric has anxiety and feels uncomfortable in social situations, so he overshares. At work, Cedric tells everyone about his medical problems, including hemorrhoids and irritable bowel. Around casual acquaintances, he talks freely about sex and asks questions about others' experiences. He asks to try other people's drinks. Cedric is very open about things he has uncovered about his relationship with his mother in psychotherapy.

Cedric overshares, and this is a boundary violation. You may be surprised to consider oversharing as a boundary violation, yet people can't unhear things that have been said. They may not want to hear those things. Having intimate knowledge that you don't want about someone affects how you see and interact with that person going forward.

Keep in mind that just because you want to share intimate information doesn't mean that other people around you feel comfortable listening. It's a good practice to check

in first. In fact, if the information is heavy or personal, I

like to ask the person I am speaking with if now is a good

time to talk about it. This allows the other person to suggest

a better time if necessary.

Communication is a two-way street. If you are only

thinking about your part, you are missing the 50 percent of

the receiving end. Oversharing makes other people

uncomfortable. Even if you are fine with giving the

information, that does not mean others want to receive it.

Stirring the Pot

No judgment here, but do you ever find yourself stirring the pot while also being aware that it is the wrong thing to do? Maybe you are bored. Maybe you are trying to divert attention from your own misdeeds onto someone else's foolishness. Perhaps you are one-upping a sibling. As humans, we sometimes find ourselves doing things that aren't healthy (and are not even aware of it), but as we've already established, humans are far from perfect.

Stirring the pot is when you start drama that doesn't need to be started or when you see drama and jump in the mix with fuel for the fire.

Parvati's mother was nagging her about finding a better job. It was a stale conversation that was painful and seemingly without end. Parvati found herself asking her mother if she knew who Parvati's brother was dating. She knew her brother was dating someone their mom would not like. She also knew that her brother didn't want their mom to know. Technically, Parvati was not betraying her brother. She was simply changing the topic of conversation by stirring the pot so her mom would stop pestering her.

Taylor, Mark, Lauren, and Keith were having a couple's game night. Keith was bored and didn't want to go in the first place. He threw out that a new person started working this week at the business where Mark also worked, and she was "mighty hot." Lauren, Keith's wife, sidestepped the trap by ignoring the comment. Taylor, on the other hand, had a history of being incredibly jealous and laid into Mark for not telling her. They began fighting, and game night was effectively over.

Sometimes people stir the pot because it is just what they do. They are heat-seeking missiles for drama. Other people do it to change the direction or focus of an interaction. Still, others have no clue that they are stirring the pot or why.

There is no need to stir the pot on purpose if you actually address what is going on in a more direct way. If there is conflict, address it. If you are bored, find something productive to do. Don't throw someone under the bus or create drama that doesn't need to be created as a means to satisfy your entertainment needs. If you want drama, watch *Succession*. If you want action, get up and move. If you want attention, take a provocative selfie. Just get your hands off the spoon.

In Fact, Ditch the Drama

The theatrics of the shitshow are everywhere. Why? Because we are humans, and the drama is baked in. One person sees it this way. Another sees it that way. Yet another sees it differently altogether. We have baggage, history, and experiences that shape our views. Some folks mesh. Some don't.

Our job is to choose which dramas we want to be a part of and which to walk away from. You may be one of those people who regularly find themselves immersed in theatrics. It may be a result of everyone bringing problems to you. It may be that you invite it—just sayin.

If you don't like drama, stop complaining about it and walk away. Stop laying out the welcome mat for people to bring their drama to you, and start giving messages that you are not going to listen open-endedly. How?

Try these responses on for size:

- I get really worked up when I hear your stories. I am not able to shut my mind off. I think I need a break.

- Wow. Have you thought about consulting a therapist to help you sort this out? I'm no professional.

- (Interrupt the trajectory of the conversation with a change of subject.) OMG. Did you see the staff meeting agenda?

- I wish I had a solution. I've got a lot of my own concerns that keep me up at night. (Moving on...)

- I've got a super busy day. I've gotta run!

- (Don't even answer the phone.)

There is no way to completely eliminate drama, but if you seriously don't like it, do something to reduce it. You have a role in creating expectations. Dealing with others' drama does serve a role in distracting you from your own shitshow. If this is the case, it's better to look at your life and what you can do to make it better so you don't want to be distracted from it quite so much.

Leave the emotional productions for the movies.

Peacemaking or Distress Intolerance?

If you're like most people, you hate conflict. It is probably somewhat in our evolution to be peacekeepers. Imagine if we made war all the time. We might actually all kill each other. While I know that recent times have felt like conflict on steroids, it is helpful to keep in mind that this has been the case throughout history. In the past, it was much more likely that a person would kill someone for not sharing the same beliefs and typically wouldn't be punished for it. I say none of this to downplay recent violence and turmoil rampant in our society.

Discord is inevitable, but I don't necessarily see conflict as bad. I view conflict more as required, necessary, and a part of human diversity. According to Dictionary.com (accessed June 11, 2023), a conflict is a disagreement. To be in conflict is to be contradictory, in opposition, or at odds. I don't know any way to exist in a world where individuality and individual differences exist and where there will not be contradictions or disagreements. I see that as normal and healthy. What is not useful is to see conflict as bad, wrong, or disordered because there is a concomitant desire to quash the tension.

As I mentioned, I think the drive to reduce conflict is understandable. It is uncomfortable, and at times, there is worry that it will escalate. Sometimes we have violent histories, and even mild clashes can be a reminder of trauma, abuse, or bad outcomes. Yet, not all conflict is violent.

The boundaries around peacemaking are really about coming to terms with co-existing with conflict. Healthy boundaries are about self-protection while also allowing disagreements to happen. It is having self-awareness around things that activate us and being intentional about how one chooses to handle the conflict. It may be that a person chooses to walk away in order to have peace. Alternatively, they may choose to let a conflict play out, recognizing that growth may happen. In some instances, it may be about just speaking one's mind and moving on. The boundary is the recognition that peacemaking may not be possible and the insistence that it may be more about your own history than it is about the parties in conflict. A goal of eradicating conflict is a self-defeating one.

The Company You Keep

If you feel beaten down, it is time to take a look around at the company you keep. As humans, our social circle has a huge impact on our mood and behavior.

Yule hates his job, and so do all of his coworkers. In fact, they have lunch together every day and trauma bond over toxic behavior in the workplace. Yule's mother has a negative outlook on life, especially since her husband died, and she calls Yule daily to complain about things that need to be done around the house and how lonely she feels. Yule has tried to get her to see a therapist, but she refuses. She calls him instead. His best friend is his brother, and they spend most of their time complaining about their mom and who has it worse with her. Yule is feeling down on life. He doesn't feel appreciated, has no energy, and spends most evenings on the couch with his roommate, drinking beer and playing video games.

People are often surprised when I recommend simple interventions like distancing from too much negativity. To be clear, I am not suggesting that you have to cut off all your relationships with people who aren't rainbows and sunshine. I am saying that if most or all of your network is laced with pessimism, the after-effect will show in your mood. While it is healthy to have someone to vent to, there is a point at which too much venting becomes rumination. Rumination is reviewing the same shit over and over with no change or benefit. People can feel like they are drowning in rumination because there is no end, and it becomes impossible to see a way out of the negative mindset. Research has even shown that support groups one-dimensionally focused on what is wrong won't show benefit compared to groups that also include some kind of problem-solving or benefit-finding.

It is also important to have others in your life who see your value and express appreciation, both at work and at home. Maybe people around you take you for granted, and maybe you have given the message that that is okay. No one likes to ask for appreciation, but allowing others to appreciate you is good for them. It is also good for you because it feels nice.

If you notice that you are feeling blah, unappreciated, or downright negative, take a good look around. I understand that sometimes we have to spend time in places that don't bring us joy, like work, but we can be more thoughtful about who we spend time with. Trauma-bonding also only goes so far before it, too, feels toxic. When you have to spend time in toxic environments, be sure to offset it with more positive experiences. Spend time doing things that make you happy. While there are a lot of things you can't control, you can influence the energy around you. Change it up, and see what happens.

Can't Touch This

The headlines over the last few years have been quite empowering around bodily space. Who knew that you shouldn't touch or be touched in the workplace without permission? In case you haven't heard, your body is your personal space. No one should be touching it without your permission. I say this fully recognizing that people have different levels of comfort around personal space and touch, and not everyone who is touchy-feely is on a mission to cop a sexual thrill. That being said, you do not have to suffer people who are hands-touching you when you are a hands-off kind of person. (Refer back to the platinum rule.)

I've been very open with my personal biases. This is one of mine. I don't really like uninvited touch. I can do a handshake (if people are even doing that anymore, given COVID-19), but I am noticing the older I get, the more handshakes hurt. People squeeze a little too hard, like they are trying to show me how easily they can crush my hand.

One person's preference to touch should never override another person's preference to not be touched, but there is no way of knowing touch preference unless you talk about it. Therefore, I recommend that you never lay hands on another person unless that person has made clear that touch is welcome. I can't think of many circumstances where your touch is necessary as a rule, unless you are giving CPR because someone isn't breathing or applying the Heimlich maneuver when someone is choking. So, it should be easy to make it a habit to keep your hands to yourself.

While you may think I am being nitpicky here, the fact of the matter is that you don't know another person's trauma history, experience with touch, or sensitivities. Your intention is irrelevant here because it is generally a personal invasion of space. In fact, better yet, make it a habit to keep a couple of feet apart unless there is a valid reason otherwise.

If someone consistently places hands (or, even worse, lips) on you in ways that you do not like, you also need to say something. I get that this will be uncomfortable, and perhaps you feel like you should not *have* to say something. But if it keeps happening, apparently you *do* have to say something. That something could be: "Hey, I'm not really a touchy-feely kind of person," "I am not comfortable with that," "In my culture, we don't do that," "It doesn't feel good when you touch me," "Keep your fucking hands to yourself," or "I've got this crazy hand rash going on!"

Some people prefer a more subtle approach, like stepping aside or shifting so contact is averted. Regardless of the method you choose, know that you have the absolute right to decide who touches you, and you do not have the right to touch others without permission. This philosophy also extends to commenting on someone's weight or general appearance. I really struggle with this as I like to give compliments or check in when someone looks tired. I don't know that there is a one-size-fits-all rule here. It probably depends on how well you know a person, and the workplace is usually best treated more conservatively. When in doubt, close your mouth and put your hands in your pockets.

Gossip

Gossip is like fudge or smooth liquor. You tell yourself that will only imbibe a little. You realize it could end badly, but hey, your intentions are good. In fact, gossip did have the historically important function of connecting marginalized groups, so it doesn't always come from a bad place. The problem these days is when the line between cohesion and innocent laughter and feeling like you're going to throw up becomes blurry. You often don't know you've crossed it until it's too late.

The allure of gossip is that it is a soap opera-like distraction from our own shitshow lives. Assuming that you are not engaging in gossip about friends and people you love, it can seem so removed from your life that it is an escape. (If you are gossiping about people whom you supposedly care about, that is another and much larger issue entirely.) In some respects, it helps us feel less screwed up to dish about other people's dirty laundry. I'm gonna be honest: I think some gossip is human—not humans at their best but a sometimes necessary part of the flawed package.

It's more of a volume concern. The more you gossip, the uglier it gets. For one, you are taking way too much pleasure in sharing other people's dirty laundry. This is not an admirable quality. A little gossip at a lunch about the goings-on at work is one thing; it is entirely different to play telephone with your entire social network.

The next point of contention is that too much gossip screams to others that you have loose lips and enjoy other people's troubles a bit too much. It's a character issue. People will rightly second-guess trusting you with personal issues going forward lest they be the subject of tomorrow's gossip train.

Then there is the issue of being so distracted by other people's issues that you avoid your own. It isn't a contest. If other people have drama going on, it doesn't somehow make yours any less important. It's not a legitimate excuse to overlook your own mess.

Lastly, I think too much gossip just makes people feel lousy. At some level, we know that it isn't becoming, and we feel a tinge guilty even as we are doing it. There is also the potential to fall into the trap of doing it more and more until your relationships are all about gossip, and then they don't feel good either.

Draw some boundaries around gossip. A little is okay as long as you aren't betraying confidences and friendships. Too much gossip will make you feel small and petty. This is one area where no one else is doing it to you. You have the power to not participate.

Why Buy the Cow When You Can Get the Milk for Free?

I used to work as a typist for a pediatrician who liked to joke with me about dating. He would say, "Remember, Jodie, why buy the cow when you can get the milk for free?" (We had this kind of trash-talking relationship. It was a different time.)

I have often invoked this phrase, but not in the context that he suggested. I apply the lesson to the world of work, a situation much more likely to involve exploitation.

It seems no matter where you are employed, the workplace will take all you are willing to give without consideration of payment. In some respects, you can't blame them. If you could get someone to work for you for free, you might consider it, especially if it were on a willing basis!

Too often, people are feeling overworked to the point of exhaustion. They feel compelled to do the work because they tell themselves that no one else will do it; work *needs* them.

Maybe. More often, though, we create scenarios, real or imagined, where work cannot do without us. It's just as likely that work doesn't have to find someone else to do the tasks as long as we are there to get it done. Why change things long-term when you give away your time so freely? The time is yours to give, after all.

Dustin was on the leadership team, and he sacrificed leisure and family for work, telling himself that he was needed. He considered himself to have a special status because of how much time and energy he dedicated to work. When I asked if it was worth the tradeoff, Dustin believed it was because he received company loyalty in exchange. He expected big promotions in the future. One day, a multi-million-dollar mistake was found, and Dustin was questioned by senior leaders who blamed him for not catching it earlier. Dustin was shocked, as he didn't make the mistake, and he felt resentful for being made a scapegoat. The loyalty he thought he had was gone in an instant. Dustin was severed.

Chew on that for a minute. Freely giving all you have to work with only a theoretical payout is a shaky investment.

If you are waiting for work to come to you and tell you to take it easy, take care of your personal needs, and stop making so many sacrifices for your job, you will be in perpetual waiting mode. It isn't going to happen because it isn't in the best interest of work for you to do so.

Boundaries are about recognizing your time, attention, and efforts as precious resources. You don't have to wait for someone to tell you they have the utmost worth. There is no incentive or bonus for that. It is a gift that you give yourself.

Check Your Political Agitation at the Door

There was a time in the recent past when I felt so incredibly demoralized by political divisions that I found myself as close as I have ever been to depression. It wasn't until I read some books on history, particularly those about the prominent leaders in the era when our country was founded, that I realized that in the US, political mudslinging has always been the norm. While I thought we had evolved in terms of couth and respectful discourse, I was either wrong or we've gone backward.

I am aware of my desire to recommend that we avoid political discussions in mixed company altogether, but I recognize this longing is fantastical. These days, asking how a person is doing is an absolute reference to politics in terms of actual threats to groups of people, their rights, livelihoods, and safety.

My admonition here is around the need to inject political ideology into *every* discussion without considering the audience or space. I am objecting to people who push a political agenda like it is a religion with a goal of converting others. I find it condescending to assume I need or want to hear unsolicited opinions on important issues that affect my well-being. Beyond this, there is consideration of ruining an otherwise enjoyable moment.

I may be at a party, dinner, or holiday event and things are going swimmingly, when someone interjects a political headline with commentary in what seems to be an attempt to infuse agitation or drama. I am speaking about intention here, where it feels like the point is to evangelize. I feel the same way when I enter a place of business or a party and a politically polarizing program is playing in the background. It feels presumptuous and, at the very least, disrespectful to guests.

The psychologist in me is deeply saddened that we can no longer even agree upon truths, and the scientist in me views this as intentional and strategic by those in power. We no longer view one another as humans but as enemies, which reminds me of the Muzafer Sherif Robbers Cave Experiment from the 1950s.[5] Sherif separated boys into groups and introduced competition for resources, which escalated into serious aggression, prejudice, and discrimination. The concept is similar to that described in Sir William Golding's 1954 book, *Lord of the Flies*. Based on science, we know how easy it is to create destructive conflict by pitting groups of people against one another through the suggestion that winning is survival. The only way out of such dilemmas is to have a shared, common goal, and I recognize this will only come about through human relationships and connection.

I don't claim to know how to accomplish this deeper social connection as immediately as we need it, but I believe it starts with approaching social situations with a bit more caution and humility. Check your need to convince, judge, and argue with others. Consider that others have the right not to be assaulted by your pontification when they are trying to enjoy themselves. At least, have some consideration beyond your own interests and preferences.

In the United States, we have hard-won rights to have opinions and to be able to express them. I am merely suggesting that you first ask if you *need* to do so, what the benefit is, what your goal is, and if this is the right time and place. The tone of a conversation about politics should not be conversion, power, and dominance. What if, instead, we spoke with an air of respect and listened a bit more? Might we come one step closer to empathy, selflessness, and enlightened connection? Is it too wild to ask humans to act beyond self-interest? I'm still holding onto hope.

Take off the Social Handcuffs

Social roles are those functions for which society has defined norms. Pay attention to the important part of this definition. Society has defined, otherwise stated, dictated. I have several questions here. Who is society? And what happens when society changes?

What I am getting at is that, yes, there are social norms that seek to create order. For example, I don't run around naked in public. Not only is it against the law, but it is frowned upon in many societies. I can see how it could cause chaos, wrecks, confusion, and fear. The problem is when social roles are applied too widely and too oppressively and when social roles and norms seek to keep certain groups in boxes as a means of control. Don't get me wrong; there are benefits to social norms, like respect, courtesy, and kindness. What do we do, however, when people slotted in certain roles don't want to live in them anymore? Not that many years ago, it was a social norm for a woman to function as keeper of the home in a full-time, unpaid job. And, children were allowed to work as low-paid laborers instead of attending school. Times have changed. Humanity has evolved.

I get a little prickly when I think of groups of people telling other groups of people how to act, look, or be. I get a lot prickly around groups of people shaming and judging other groups based on norms they have chosen to live by, as if everyone else should, too. That's not the way life works. We make our own life choices, but why should we give ourselves permission to make life choices for other people simply because we believe we know better, have higher moral standards, and have the power to impose them?

Of course, there need to be some limits. Even if all people don't share the value of not stealing, we still need rules against stealing and not molesting children and not driving under the influence of impairing substances. We can still have some basic expectations with reasonable interpretations that don't involve imposing personal value systems on others. What I can't seem to grasp is why others should be mandating to other people how to live their personal lives.

Evolution is change that happens over time under the umbrella of ensuring survival. Social roles and norms similarly have evolved. That is healthy, even if it is uncomfortable, but it doesn't have to be personal. If you choose not to change, that is your right. It is not your right to choose for others. It's time to take off the handcuffs of social roles and begin to ask ourselves what feels right in our own lives. In what ways have we absorbed values that aren't a good fit for us? Cut the chains. Give yourself permissions to be free!

Keeping Up with the Joneses

Social comparison has some good functions. It sometimes helps us elevate our performance to compare ourselves to others. It can also help us feel grateful for what we have, particularly if we are doing better than others. The downside of evaluating ourselves next to others is feeling the need to keep up and telling ourselves that we are less than if we don't.

The need to keep up with our neighbors and what they have and what they are doing can become a prison: We feel we are not good enough and have to earn approval through the accumulation of stuff, wealth, and experiences. The real trap is feeling our worth is measured by these external standards.

I once worked with Joe, who had a great job with a nice salary. As time went by, Joe found that what was once considered great had degraded into inadequacy. Through pressure from his family, he now felt they had to join a certain club, move to a certain neighborhood, spend a certain amount of money there, drive a certain car, have parties with certain food and experiences, go on certain vacations, and have certain hobbies. Joe, who had once worked to enjoy his life, now worked endlessly to afford his life, and now he was falling behind in that. A once generous income was no longer enough, and he began to feel like a failure. In fact, Joe felt like a sham. He didn't deserve to hang out in the exclusive friend group because he believed he didn't belong there, and socializing had lost its luster anyway due to his feeling not good enough. Joe felt more and more isolated. He tried to tell his partner how he felt, but his partner was knee-deep in the social strata. Joe was afraid of being rejected. He didn't want to take away from his family what his hard work had afforded them. Joe began to feel that his lifestyle was an albatross, and depression set in.

I explained to Joe that he had fallen into a rabbit hole that consumed many other people in the United States, but there was a way out. That is to let it all go. If he had to buy his way into a friend group, then it wasn't really a friend group. If friends judged him for driving an economy car, they weren't really the friends he wanted. Unless he knew that he was being judged by others for a certainty, he was also being judgmental himself. I suspected that there were others in the friend group who had the same struggles as Joe, but they, too, were afraid to be different. In some ways, adulthood can have some of the same trappings as adolescence, particularly if we never learned how to navigate them as a teenager. Life presents the same lessons over and over until we learn them. Only then can we go on to the next one.

Keeping up with social cliques is a high-school game, and it's really predictably boring. Everyone is the same, does the same thing, and acts the same way. It looks good from the outside, but the inside is really a prison.

Have the courage to step outside and feel comfortable; that

is a freer, more beautiful place to be. Others will likely join

you, and if they don't, maybe it's because they were the

prison guards, after all.

Fuck the Influencers

Admittedly, I have a strong distaste for the concept of superficial influencing. I am talking about influencing clothing trends, beauty trends, and what's in or out. I have a bit of an ornery streak. Once I learn something is in, I reject or resist it until it is no longer in. Then, I might try it.

Why? I think it has to do with pushing back against people telling me what is cool and what isn't cool and implying that it is important for me to keep up in order to be included or cool or well thought of. I mean, who gets to decide? Admittedly, I'm a control freak. That's my real issue, and it seems a bit pretentious to have the power to tell others what is hip. Then again, I own that I am not trendy, so if you want to be fashionable, you probably shouldn't follow my lead here.

I don't have anything against influencers in general. Everyone has to make a living, and I admire the achievements of culling a following, which isn't as easy as one might think. It's just that I rebel against the idea of anyone being overly influential and feeling the need to chase fads as a way to feel worthwhile. Maybe even more deeply, I see influencing as a personalized way to market products. It is advertising on the down-low disguised as trend-setting.

Underneath the pull to closely follow influencers, I think, is a desire to fit in or achieve a sense of worth. Stable self-worth is not something that will ever be attained by how you look, what you wear, and what you have. Healthy self-worth comes from within and often has to do much more with deeply held values, doing for others, a giving nature, and contributing beyond one's personal self-interest.

Looking to someone else who doesn't even know you for input on what you should do to conform to the latest trends is okay for a personal interest, but it can easily take over your mind. Looking to see what the influencers say, suggest, or approve, you can lose track of your own personal compass or style.

As a society, we have gotten way out of hand with this influencing and advertising business. Just look at your electronic news feed. On mine, I can track the latest weight loss trends, food fads, workout routines, and medical testing I should do. For the longest time, I had guidance on vaginal rejuvenation in my feed. Does a person really need vaginal rejuvenation? The topic would not have been top (or even bottom) of mind on any particular day for me, but the frequency I was told that it would improve my quality of life suggests high importance.

When you get to be my age, you will also notice that once you do all of these things you are being encouraged to do, it will all change—sometimes back to a previous trend—such that you will always be chasing a trend. What is in must continually change to keep us hooked. One month, I might be drinking red wine for my heart. The next month, I am told I should never drink red wine because I will get cancer. I should be into the dry life because I can lose a ton of weight that way. WTF?

Marketing is meant to sway all of us because it leads to profit. Set some boundaries around access to your psyche, and remind yourself that marketing is designed to control you by making you feel less than or in need of an enhancement to be worthy. Be intentional about what you choose to follow, and know that the smoke and mirrors are there so you never really know what is real. Indeed, real is being turned into what you absolutely should never want.

People-Pleasing and the Road to Nowhere

Here is the deal. If you are always pleasing other people, and other people have different standards, who are you really? What is authentic? What if you are in a room with two very different people who have very different standards? Can you please both? How do you decide?

Phoebe was absolutely exhausted. When she described a typical week, it was easy to see why. At work, she got a sense of accomplishment from making people happy, so she rarely said, "No." This was a double-edged sword because, while this pleased others, she often felt she was drowning. When she got home, she had to make a few different meals to please the different preferences of her kids. Since her divorce, she worried excessively about keeping the kids happy when they spent time at her house. Her friends complained that she never had time to hang out. They nagged her to join them on adventures when she felt too tired to go, and she went anyway because she didn't want to let them down. Phoebe had no space in her life for herself; she was too busy juggling the preferences and priorities of other people.

People-pleasing is a lose-lose scenario. Statistically, you just can't do it. It is not possible. At any given time, 50 percent of people won't like you, and that's okay because it's a fact of life. Some days it rains. Not every day is sunny. That is a good thing. You don't like half the people you meet. Does that make them bad people? I hope not. We all have preferences. Maybe you like quiet people. Does that make talkative people bad? Maybe you find tall attractive. Does that make short people off-putting?

Difference is inherent in society. It is what will help us survive as a species. We cannot please multiple masters, and the most important authority is our selves. When we are so busy earning approval from others, we lose sight of what we really want. We lose sight of our selves. There is no one to please us, and sometimes we don't even know who we are as a result.

Although you may have been taught that what other people think is supremely important, that is wildly untrue. People use that idea to control you, and that is a big problem. Giving you approval makes you jump. Withholding it also makes you jump. Do you think others don't know that about you?

Sadly, the tendency toward people-pleasing doesn't go away just because you notice it. At the same time, noticing it gives you great power. You can actively show up and ask yourself if you really want to go there. Are you just reacting? Is this what you want to do? Where is your personal perspective in the situation?

The people who are with you only to control you will suddenly not want to be around you anymore. That's completely fine because why would you want to surround yourself with people who don't accept you for the person you are, instead of those who give you unconditional acceptance? Now, while I may not love 100 percent of the qualities in someone, I can still accept them. That one annoying thing doesn't ruin the person (most of the time). However, if I am invested in using someone, I will begin looking for my next target to please me. I get it. It's great to be surrounded by people who are into making me happy; it means less work for me. It isn't a super satisfying place for the person on the other end, though.

Do yourself a favor. Get generous with the fuck-offs in your head. When you find yourself overly concerned with someone else's happiness, remind yourself that it is the other person's problem. When you find yourself concerned with how someone else perceives you, remind yourself that, too, is the other person's problem. When you find that being your own person pushes people away, drop a "good riddance" under your breath, and breathe in the influx of air.

The Truth About Work

For many of us, our work ethic, career, or vocation is central to our identity. This is why it is so easy to fall into the trap of working ourselves out of a personal life. The ensnarement—beyond that of running oneself ragged—is based on the lie that we tell ourselves, which is that we will get caught up *eventually*. This may have once been true, but sadly, in today's world, there will just be more work. *There* or *done* do not exist. Clearing out your to-do pile only makes room for more work.

The questions are: Do you know the difference between work and not work? Are you being honest with yourself about what must be done versus what you feel should be done? At some point, there needs to be a dividing line or work will simply take over life. If we are going to be happy, we must be candid with ourselves about deciding where that line will be, *as if* we have a choice, because we do have a choice. You see, it is too easy to surrender choice to emotional reactions—guilt, compulsiveness, people-pleasing. We can tell ourselves that we have no control, which leads to feelings of victimization and helplessness. These are lies. It is important to understand that each time we make more time for work, we are saying no to something else in our lives. It is, indeed, a zero-sum game.

Suellyn worked in finance. Her typical workweek was sixty hours. On weekends, she just wanted to sleep. She was too physically and emotionally exhausted to engage, but she was still lonely. This pattern destroyed her romantic and social life. What kept Suellyn engaged was the promise of promotion to vice president, and she'd all but been told that the job was hers. Once she got the promotion, she promised herself that she would chill a little. The problem was that the economy had been so volatile that there seemed to be a new crisis every day. Suellyn was always in catastrophe mode, and her boss kept hinting that how she handled the pressure was being observed.

Things culminated, and Suellyn was not well-prepared for a big meeting. Everything turned out okay, but she looked a little rusty. Her boss met with her and said they were choosing to promote someone else. Suellyn fought for herself, listing all the things she had accomplished and sacrificed, but the deal was done. Suellyn felt stabbed in the back, both by her boss and by herself. She told herself she was sacrificing for the promise of a reward, but there was no recovering lost time. It was all a shell game.

The boundary has to be set within ourselves because we cannot expect work to tell us we have done enough. The red line is stopping the fucked up lies and compulsions to do more. It is ending the nonsense *shoulds, have to's*, and *musts*. While it may feel like certain things have to get done, feelings are not rational and can sometimes be more about early life programming than the actual tasks before you. At the end of the day, will getting that report done really matter—more than your happiness, time with family and friends, more than your emotional and physical health? While there is much that you cannot control at work, you do get to control your mindset. Never let them take your mind.

Bonus Section: Expert's Guide to Setting a Boundary at Work

What I am going to describe now is such an exquisite use of a boundary that it is an art form and worthy of a special section. When I first heard about it, I recognized its brilliance immediately, and I feel compelled to share it even though it is a bit deviant.

My niece just started graduate school, and she requested a meeting with her assigned mentor to discuss some ideas for her capstone project. She wanted to ask questions to make sure she was on the right track before she put in too much work on the high-stakes assignment. My niece was also eager and excited. Why not make use of someone who was tasked with mentoring her?

She emailed her mentor and asked for an appointment to discuss the capstone project. Her mentor replied, "SWOT it out, and if you still have questions, let me know." My niece was a bit stunned and called me to ask what I thought about this response. She asked if this was normal in grad school.

In retrospect, I believe I laughed out loud—both with humor and some level of appreciation of this master-level boundary application.

SWOT stands for Strengths, Weaknesses, Opportunities, and Threats. I first learned about the technique when I worked in graduate medical education. We would often sit as a group and make comprehensive lists of strengths, weaknesses, opportunities, and threats for proposed projects or changes within the organization. The benefit of a SWOT analysis is that it provides a systematic method to examine issues from multiple angles so that a team can develop the most effective plan based on data.

I told my niece that her mentor had essentially said, "Fuck off and stop bothering me." While this was highly inappropriate for a mentor to do, especially when one considers the cost of graduate school, I could absolutely appreciate the eloquence of this boundary-setting skill in work situations. The fundamental message was *Figure it out on your own before bothering me with pesky questions*, but the mentor did so in a way that superficially appeared legit. (It was not actually justifiable because it was the mentor's job to mentor.) It threw my niece off balance.

I have added SWOT it out to my professional boundary toolbox, and maybe you should add it to your workplace toolbox for the next time a colleague asks you to do work that isn't yours to do. It is a great tool when used appropriately. It's a super nice way of saying, *Go right on over there and fuck off already.*

Incivility—The Pig in Slop

These days, incivility seems to be the standard operating procedure, which is unfortunate because it is bottom-barrel behavior. Incivility refers to rude and disrespectful behavior, which should be embarrassing but, sadly, is becoming normalized in our dehumanizing social discourse. Incivility refers to when we begin to treat others as if they are non-human, machine-like, or somehow cut off from feeling.

Social media has set off incivility like an accelerant. Our comfort with electronic communication allows us to view one another as if we are simply computers. We are too easily detached from the idea that there is a living, breathing human on the other end. Our feedback is no longer entirely constructive but sometimes intent on being so direct that we cut the person on the receiving end to the core. We fire off cruel remarks, which if hurled at us, would crush our souls. We are so disconnected from humanity that we are becoming the very thing we rail against.

You can't control what other people do, but you can hold your own conduct to a higher standard, meaning you can choose not to wrestle with the pig. There is no better response to a nasty, dull-minded person than no response. No response gives them nothing to come back against. It communicates that you are above the pigsty. You are saying that you are above engaging.

As I type this, I recognize that one response style doesn't fit all situations. There are times when you do have to stand up and defend yourself, particularly if someone is being abusive. I am suggesting that you intentionally decide those times instead of impulsively engaging with the dumbassery before it spills onto you.

A handful of times on my social media, someone has made a snarky or outright mean-spirited comment that I have analyzed for hours, trying to understand. Repeatedly, I started to reply and then deleted it until I forgot due to other distractions. A lack of time ended the dilemma. I was the only one stuck on it anyway. I have since chosen not to consider such bullshit, and I am healthier for it.

Check yourself next time you want to shoot off some snark. Is this the kind of person you want to be, or is this the person you are goaded into becoming? Let the other person know you are not getting on their level. Give up the immediate rush you would get from the self-indulgence of incivility, and remind yourself that there is a human at the other end of the equation.

Threats to Humanity

In early 2020, during the stay-home phase of COVID-19, I shopped for groceries once a week. If it hadn't been such a scary time, it would have made an interesting study: Some people weren't wearing masks, others were, and a few were wearing full-on gas masks. Because it was hard to see folks' faces, it was difficult to read expressions, but I could see the wild-eyed looks of discomfort that arose when others got too close. People looked at one another as threats. Perhaps it was a fear of catching the disease or only the presence of a rival for scarce toilet paper or flour. I felt that we saw one another as the enemy. Politics set all of that on fire, and what was an infectious disease became a cancer.

During this time, my phone started blowing up with people, particularly teenagers, needing someone to talk with about anxiety. They seemed to struggle the most with losing contact with friends and social routines. I also had a spike in calls from folks I'd seen in the distant past for anxiety, which made an aggressive resurgence—folks who were worried they would die and couldn't stop overthinking. They didn't know what to do. Many were emotionally eating and using substances to self-soothe. This turned out to be a national trend.

In some ways, I think we were doing the best that we could at the time with what we knew. I get annoyed when folks act as if they had the answer. No one knew what the hell was going on. It was a shitshow. It's too easy to feel, with the new information we gained over time, that the solution was straightforward. The bigger issue is that we turned on one another, or at least those people who thought they had the answers turned on others. If it all happened again, I don't even know if people would handle it any differently.

If we are going to survive as a species, a point which is in doubt, we are going to have to draw some boundaries around fear and existential threats. Yes, COVID-19 killed millions, and it was real. It was scary. We had to do something. No, I don't think we can force others to do our will. We have to let that go. No, it isn't ideal. At the same time, how much do we attend to the very real risk we face every damned day getting into a car? Our risk of dying is associated with a car accident more than it is with any other outside threat, assuming you aren't in the active military serving in a war zone. How much thought do we give auto accidents when we are trying to text and drive or are messing with technology behind the wheel? How much thought do we give our health and well-being when we pollute our one and only water supply, which surely increases cancer? How much do we consider the junk we pour into our bodies when the number-one killer of adults is heart disease?

Fear is related to what we attend to, and that usually is the loudest, most aggressive threat. During the height of the pandemic, the threat of the virus was the only thing on the news. Despite the fact that we need each other to survive, the pandemic turned into a free-for-all where we saw our neighbors as the enemy, which will do nothing for survival. The anxiety alone takes away any chance at peace. We begin to make ourselves sick.

I submit to you that the biggest threat to our health, wellness, and survival is fear—fear of change, fear of difference, fear of each other. Fear without rational analysis is inherently unhinged, but we choose to allow it to take over and drive us to irrational behavior. Fear fools us into believing the loudest and most confident voice in the room, even if that voice is spewing nothing more than drivel. We cling to certainty to quell the fear, and this will continue to be our downfall. Other biological and conflictual existential threats will come. There is no need to create them in our minds. Doing so just makes it more likely that we will kill each other. That is what fear does.

BOUNDARIES WITH OTHER

PAINS IN THE ASS (OR MIND)

Non-Acceptance of Reality

There is a famous idiom, "Keep your friends close; keep your enemies closer," which surprisingly underscores the importance of acceptance. It is better to have a close relationship with your enemies so you know what they are doing. In everyday life, there is much that we don't want to accept—illness, racism, poverty, incivility—because these things are painful to face. Yet, if we don't acknowledge their existence, we cannot do anything meaningful to change them.

I once worked with a Black senior executive who told me that she welcomed honest opinions about diversity, even if they were overtly racist. I said to her that they must be incredibly hard to hear, especially when they are personal to her. She replied that she cannot begin to make a realistic plan to combat misconceptions or racist attitudes until she creates a space for them to be identified. Somehow, this incredible woman was able to depersonalize something I imagine feels like an individual attack. I don't pretend to fully understand how she was able to do this, but I respect the hell out of it because she has a point. It is easier to address something that you can overtly identify.

Non-acceptance is essentially denial of reality. I get it. There are some things we just don't want to face, but avoidance doesn't change reality. It just prolongs the pain. We have to set boundaries with ourselves around the fairytales we tell ourselves that don't match reality. We have to set boundaries with others who refuse to accept the way we live our lives and the boundaries we set. Both of these boundaries—with self and others—are about getting on with the business of reality and all the pain that comes with it so that we stand a better shot at making the difference we seek.

Non-acceptance prevents us from growing and being effective. It allows the enemy to grow and become even more powerful. The enemy in the shadows moves about unmonitored and stealthy and may end up biting you

in the ass.

Manipulation

That word sounds so negative and dirty. While I get that manipulation can be intentionally exploitative and destructive, I tend to view it more neutrally. I'm creative that way.

According to Dictionary.com, manipulation is the act of manipulating. (This definition is not helpful.) Manipulating is further defined as "to manage or influence skillfully." Strictly interpreted, this sounds healthy and positive. When people use manipulation unfairly or in a coercive manner, it's toxic. This can be a fine line. Reality dictates that people are invested in certain outcomes. Call it human nature. We want what we want. At the same time, others want what they want. What happens when these wants are in opposition to one another? Answer: Manipulation sometimes happens. This is why we cannot allow others' agendas to rule our lives—in doing so, our own needs never get met. There's no point getting all up in arms about it. We can simply recognize that everyone has their own needs and wants, which coexist with ours. Each of us must focus on our own shit. Sometimes circumstances dictate that we focus a little more on the shit of those we love who are acting in self-defeating ways, but there are whole books on that alone.

All humans manipulate to get what we want and to meet our needs. How we manipulate—the degree we go to—is the larger issue. The intention is supremely important, but we may not be aware of our or another's intention.

Dispense with the self-inflicted wounds of judgment or victimization. They are pointless because the tension between what others request or insist upon will coexist with our own stuff. No need to make it more dramatic than it needs to be. Just set the damned boundaries.

Growth Robbery

Sometimes, we tell ourselves horror stories. We say: "If I don't do Y, bad things will happen." (Or some version of that.) I like to turn this idea on its head: "If I do Y, what *real* good will I be doing?"

When we do too much for others, we are not allowing them to learn to do for themselves. In other words, we are robbing others of growth opportunities. All growth comes from pain—or at least the zone of discomfort. We have to allow that pain to happen, even if it is excruciating to observe.

Lawrence has a brother, Kelvin, who has a spending problem, and Lawrence feels bad for him. Kelvin always struggled in school, and their parents babied him and always bailed him out of trouble. But their parents died years ago. Now, Kelvin looks to Lawrence to be his savior, and Lawrence feels conflicted. On one hand, he sees Kelvin as incredibly talented in the technology world, where

Lawrence believes that, with discipline, Kelvin can achieve more. On the other hand, Lawrence pities Kelvin for not being strong enough to manage independence. As a result, Lawrence finds himself stepping into the role of parent with Kelvin—nagging him, giving him money, and monitoring him. By doing so, Lawrence quells his anxiety in the short term, but he sees that his actions keep Kelvin in a dependent position. The crux of the matter is that Lawrence has such strong doubt about Kelvin's ability to do for himself that it is just easier to do for him, and nothing changes.

Most of us can identify with a similar dynamic with those we love. Check yourself. This is not about sadism and enjoyment of others' hurt. It is more about allowing the ache to exist for the sake of growth. If the idea of allowing others to experience pain feels too overwhelming, the cure is to pull back and stop observing so closely.

When we jump in to fix others' problems and discomfort, we are really fixing our own pain—our guilt and sadness. We tell ourselves we are intervening for the sake of the other person when, in fact, it is more about putting our own minds to rest. The boundaries to be set are internal. They are about managing the anxiety that compels us to overact. We need to invoke patience and calm to allow the pain and growth that others deserve on their journey to becoming whole. Yes, fixing others' problems is taking from them the privilege of developing their own skills, leaving them perpetually dependent. I'm guessing that's not what you are shooting for.

Givers Attract Takers

This is a law of nature. People who are super giving attract people who are super taking. It makes sense, right? If someone is a taker or a user, that person would want to be around people from whom they can take. Otherwise, there would be no reward or payoff.

The stray animals in the neighborhood only come to the houses where food is available. They aren't stupid.

Mindi is a generous, loving, happy person by nature. But lately, she finds herself exhausted and disappointed with life. This is unlike her, and she judges herself for not being more grateful. One of her adult children lives with her and isn't working. She feels awful because he is depressed and has no energy to look for a job. To get him moving, she doesn't know what to do because she doesn't want to push too hard, but at the same time, she is tired of picking up after him, doing his laundry, and giving him money.

Mindi's boyfriend is *a little selfish*. He works all day, and when he comes home, he is too tired to do anything. Mindi cooks for him and cleans up the kitchen. She does his laundry and tries hard to keep him happy. She feels she owes him that much because he gives her some money for the expenses. They used to have fun together, but he seems to be more into online porn than her these days.

Mindi's mother is getting older, and she expects Mindi to pick her up every Wednesday to go to the grocery store and run errands. Mindi *can't* tell her mother no because her mom has no one else. Mindi sucks it up here, and she judges herself for not being more appreciative that her mom is even alive.

At work, Mindi feels like she is always cleaning up others' messes, literally and figuratively. She cleans out the work refrigerator and microwave because they get so gross, and no one else seems to have time. She also finds that others frequently come to her for help on their projects. Mindi enjoys being useful, and it feels good that people seek her out, yet she feels used and unacknowledged at work.

Mindi says that even when she has time for socializing, it is not renewing. Her friends have a lot of problems, and they usually only have time to talk about their own issues, never getting around to talking about Mindi's stress. When they do, her friends tell her to kick her son out, and that feels so hurtful to hear that she avoids the topic. Mindi judges herself for feeling resentful.

Before you start pointing the finger at Mindi, be sure you take a look at your own life. Givers are people who want to help, but the drive gets out of control. It is easier to see it in someone else than in our own lives.

Ideally, human relationships are give and take. I do for you and then you want to do for me. I listen to your problems, and you listen to mine. I pick up your kids after school on Monday, and you pick up mine on Tuesday. I invite you to lunch at my house on Saturday, and you invite me to your house for dinner next month. There is a dual energy transfer.

I can't tell you how often people describe the exhaustion of not having enough energy and resources to go around. When we dig in, it becomes obvious that these people have a one-dimensional relationship with giving. They give away, but no one around them is giving back. Therefore, they never feel replenished.

These same people push back when I suggest that they are doing too much. It is what they know to do, and some of it feels really good. It has just gotten out of control. There is no return on investment.

If you are a giver by nature, I am not saying that you should change who you are. I am saying that you should consider where you invest yourself so that you use your resources in the best way. Be aware of the energy expend. Reel it in a little. Giving away your gifts to someone who is a user is a waste because it doesn't create any growth. It is not selfish at all to expect a return. In fact, I would say that expecting a return is allowing others the chance to do something that feels good, just as it feels good for us.

Save your reserve for someone who truly deserves what you have to offer. To be clear, I am not talking about caregiving for loved ones who cannot care for themselves. In this circumstance, we often want to take care of someone who has been so loving to us. Alternatively, I have met people who feel trapped in caregiving relationships that feel obligatory, abusive, and resentful. Be discerning, and prune back the relationships that are exhausting you. There is no win if you end up depleted. Then, there is nothing to give at all.

Say, "No" to Numbing

You know that feeling after a long day? You just want to check out, numb the pain, and shut down your mind. When I'm emotionally exhausted, it is too easy to have a glass of wine or to eat cake, cookies, and ice cream to ease the pain. At the same time, indulging in this kind of hedonism comes at a cost. It is like feeding the child monster (A.K.A., the emotional self) inside so it just shuts up. I don't know about you, but I feel lousy after humoring my emotional self. I end up feeling more anxious and having low energy after the crash that follows. Sugar, highly processed foods, and junk do that to you. The feel-good only lasts for a moment, and then the bill comes due.

Overextended!

What I am describing is a biological process. When humans are emotionally activated, there is a cascade of neuroendocrine responses within your body. The numbing I reference is a drive to seek some kind of external, low-hanging fruit to quell the agitation you feel or give yourself a dopamine boost. You cannot help that you feel agitated, but any immediate relief you seek is probably unhealthy.

I am not suggesting a blanket *no* to decadent food or drink or whatever indulgent thing you are seeking to feel better. I am saying to be honest and intentional about what you are doing and why you are doing it. If you are seeking to avoid some kind of pain or to numb a pain, just no. Relief will be ultra-short. The pain will still be there when you are done, and you will feel even more psychologically shitty because you will feel physically crummy.

As with most things in life, the healthier, more effective solution is the more difficult path; it will also sound completely unattractive when you need it the most, which is why the healthy choices take planning. It is not reasonable to think that a person who is emotionally exhausted, set off, or feeling a wreck will be easily able to avoid numbing in the moment without any planned alternatives.

What the hell am I talking about? I am suggesting that you discover what you really need in a jam ahead of time. Have a toolbox at the ready. Is it calling a friend? Is it taking a walk? Is it watching a trashy show? Using a foot massager, writing, or exercising? Maybe it is making yourself a healthy smoothie or reheating your favorite healthy dish, which you prepared ahead of time and is waiting in the freezer. I am guessing it is not having self-defeating food and drink within arm's reach at home.

The takeaway around numbing is that it's all about knowing when enough is enough and being clear about the end game. Are you seeking to feel better? And if so, for how long? If it is for fifteen minutes, then have more cake, but be sure to tell yourself that you haven't yet reached rock bottom.

Accept Conflicting Emotions

One thing is certain: Life is not for the faint of heart. If you are connected to the world around you, it is clear that suffering is everywhere. There is also happiness, joy, and satisfaction. The reality is that even though we may be hyper-focused on one emotion, like joy or heartbreak, multiple conflicting emotions coexist at any given time. Maybe one overrides the other, or one is more front and center. We can be happy and seemingly carefree even when there is war and poverty in the world. We can be sad even when we have a new baby. We can both feel paralytic worry and electric excitement when taking a risk.

Regardless of what emotional experience we attend to at any given moment, it is everything all at once. Emotional acceptance is allowing this to be. Acceptance does not mean that we are comfortable that pain exists in the world during our joy. It also does not mean that we don't experience moments of joy during extremely painful times or that these extremes don't coexist in the world.

For example, there may be a natural disaster that we see on television that is completely devastating for those affected and for those seeing it play out on the screen. At the same time, we may be celebrating a birth, a graduation, or a new job. Someone may die in our family, and while we are devastated, we may also be relieved. There is no need to beat yourself up about it or lay on the guilt trip.

It doesn't mean you are a bad person. I think that is what it comes down to, actually. We have these complex emotional experiences, and at the same time, we judge ourselves for having them. We fear that we may, deep down, be bad people. I am here to tell you that is complete horseshit.

Emotional acceptance is acknowledging pain as part of life without feeling the need to make it all fit neatly. Acceptance does not mean being comfortable with mediocrity or giving up. It is more about recognizing that some things in life are avoidable, and we have to allow them to be in order to decide what to do next. It is when we respond when activated without thinking that we feel and act out of control.

The boundary is saying, "No" to restrictions around which emotions are acceptable. Emotional acceptance is co-existing with things that we do not like because there is no way around it. Acceptance is making space without judgment. You may be completely pissed that you are a human being, but that is another problem altogether.

You Already Know What's in the News, and It Sucks

The news is overwhelmingly negative and filled with scary headlines. While I believe it is irresponsible not to have a clue what is going on in the world, it is very easy to become overloaded. This became an issue for me after COVID-19. I'm a news follower, but whether it was having too much time or the world just exploding, I fell into the hole of news overload, particularly politics.

What a dumpster fire. It was like being transfixed with a silent scream while my nervous system shot electric tingles throughout my body, and yet I persisted in seeking more and more. My mood spiraled, and I began to mirror the toxicity I loathed in the headlines.

I recognize that to keep news in business, there is an insatiable appetite for provocation and shock. The news is meant to stir up shit to keep you coming back for more. It is an industry with a very dark side.

I take particular offense at opinion media disguised as news. Opinion media is just that—an opinion. It is not news. Don't call it news. It is camouflaged by focusing on the credentials of those giving opinions as if they are stating facts, and it is intended to scare you because if you are afraid, you will come back for more. You will be seeking the cure for your fear, conveniently dosed by the person with the so-called expert opinion.

Don't be confused about what I am saying. There is no nuance here. Opinion media is meant to control your mind and your behavior through the infliction of terror. I say that as a psychologist and keen observer of the fever pitch I have seen in the headlines. I believe much of it is meant to create discontent, increase viewership, and influence politics. I know that information is skewed and cherry-picked to support the points being made.

Almost as bad is the rest of the news world reporting on the talking heads giving opinions as if that is newsworthy. So, even if I am not watching opinion news, I can follow all of the opinions out there within the general news media. I sure as shit don't consider that news.

Be intentional about the headlines and stories you consume. Hate is hate. If you are listening to hate (even if it is dressed up as fact or morals or religion), you will feel hate. Why in the hell would anyone be invested in stirring up the hate? Clue: To influence and control. Know your sources. Vet them. Set aside a circumscribed time to consume news (written, audio, or visual), and keep taking your emotional temperature. If you feel jacked up after consuming news, maybe you should reconsider, look for something less sensational, or just shut it the fuck off.

Social Media Is a Mindfuck

There are mounds of research studies showing that social media leads to higher rates of anxiety, depression, and feelings of social isolation. This is particularly the case among kids, who don't have the life experience to manage it all, although many of us can easily fall into the trap of comparing ourselves and measuring worth alongside fakery.

Arianda was livid when she found out that her favorite self-help author and influencer was divorcing. Arianda had been following this guru throughout the pandemic and felt ashamed because she wasn't able to replicate the sublimely spicy romantic ambiance the guru portrayed with her husband. Arianda beat herself up and began to question if her marriage was healthy because no matter what she did, the insatiable lusty passion vibes never materialized. Arianda even considered having an affair.

Then, as the pandemic eased, her idol announced she was divorcing. WTF?

I have an idea. Maybe it was never real in the first place. Real life doesn't sell on social media. It isn't sexy enough or enough of an escape from the mundane. Enter Photoshop! One reason social media fucks with our minds so much is that although it isn't real, we tell ourselves that it *could* be real. In comparison, our lives suck.

We also use social media as a way to measure our worth based on our popularity, obsessing about the number of likes or comments on posts. We stalk what other people, who always seem to be happy, doing interesting things, and being celebrated by many, are doing, and in comparison, our lives leave us feeling less than. We feel left out of activities and wonder what is wrong with us that we weren't invited. Why aren't people commenting on my posts?

Let me be clear. This is not real. This is curated bullshit. My son recently told me that if I want to get more views on social media, I need to get some clickbait headlines. He suggested, "Psychologist shares a list of her patients' names!" He then told me the post would not have anything to do with that, but I could just use it to get views. I smirked and said, "Why would I ever do that?" He replied, "It's how it works." So, essentially, I have to trick people into viewing my legit material because they would not want to view it knowing it is legit. If I trick them with something salacious, I can jack up my exposure, which then influences other people to think it is worth viewing based on the number of views.

No, thank you.

Do you see how messed up this is? Limit time and exposure on social media. It is not reality. It is not a measure of worth. It is a twisted fantasy land that allows people to escape the doldrums and anxieties of real life.

Just remember that when you are done, you will return to

real life, often with a crash landing.

Time Is THE Most Precious Resource

Somewhere in the fourth decade (and sometimes fifth), people seemingly wake up to the reality that time is limited and life is finite, and this is often associated with extreme existential discomfort.

Earlier in development, we are busy finding ourselves, discovering love, and creating the life we want. That takes a lot of time and effort, and there isn't so much energy given to noticing how fast the clock is ticking. Predictably, midlife happens, and it can be a real slap in the face to realize that half of your life is in the rearview mirror.

I am not saying that this is a bad thing. It is more of a human thing. It is hard for a younger person to comprehend the weight of appreciating the moment when there is so much more that they want to achieve. All of this is quite natural.

One of my biggest regrets in life is that I didn't appreciate some of the experiences I was having at the time because I had no understanding that I would not have them again. In some respects, I was immersed in enjoying myself, but I absolutely wished I would have been aware of fleeting time. People change. People die. We move. Life happens.

If you started treating your time as the most precious resource, you would be a lot more judicious about how you use it. You would be more selective about who you spend time with and what you spend it on. You would approach some moments with more appreciation, and you'd spend less time on self-pity because when you do, the bad moments seem to pass more quickly. Unless you are Dr. Strange-like, you probably have the same limitations as the rest of us mere humans.

It is fabulous to have opportunities, but when we overbook our lives, it becomes difficult to fully experience what we are doing when we are doing it. Days become like puzzles where we try to fit more in, and we end up running around out of control, wondering how we got here.

What I find extremely fascinating is that so many of our technological advances were meant to make life easier and give us more time, but we usually just sabotage all that by cramming more absurdity into our days. There is a benefit to being busy but not so busy that you feel overwhelmed by your to-do list.

It is time to stop running on the insane gerbil wheel—hoping, praying, crying for things to slow down— and step up to own that we play a role in how we use time. We cannot expect things to change "one day" until we manage our schedules in a thoughtful way. One day may never come, or it may come too late.

No one, and I mean no one, is guaranteed another today, another tomorrow, another minute. When we live for tomorrow, we aren't necessarily being honest with ourselves. If we lose tomorrow, the value of today shoots through the roof.

I often ask people about going on long road trips as a kid for the promise of an amazing experience at the destination. At the time, most kids viewed the ride in the car as the most excruciating part because they just wanted to get *there*. As adults, no one remembers the destination in any detail, but they absolutely remember the car ride with an unrivaled nostalgic fondness. It is not just where you are going; it is the process of getting there where all the fun lies.

Time can never be reproduced, and there are rarely do-overs. How do you want to spend this moment and the next and the next? It takes awareness but also ownership. You have a say in how you spend your time. Stop giving away and wishing away time as if it has no meaning. Stop spending it on things that don't matter in your life. Take a moment to appreciate where you are. Life is what you make it. Take time to reflect, be intentional, and plan like time is a precious resource. Live smarter. Live better. Live deeper.

Money Won't Buy Happiness

I've often thought that if I had enough money to pay off my debts, I would be happier. I note that my mind jumps to: *"Well, then I would need more money for a rainy day. I need more money for retirement and healthcare. I would need more money for my kids' education."*

The bottom line is that there will never be enough money, and yet I can be happy. I am happy even though I don't have an endless supply of the green.

At the same time, I recognize that I am incredibly fortunate. I have a home, I am healthy for now, I have a means to make a living, and I don't worry about finding my next meal.

The research on the relationship between money and happiness is ever-evolving, but money doesn't consistently predict happiness as long as you have enough to cover basic needs like housing, food, transportation, and healthcare. The amount of money needed to cover these needs is probably related to where you live. Folks who live in California likely require more money to cover basic living expenses than folks who live in rural Tennessee.

Note that I said basic *needs* and not *wants*. Needs are things you require in order to live, like food, healthcare, shelter, and medication. Wants are those things you prefer to have. My son *needs* a reliable car to get to work, so he has a Chevrolet Equinox. But, he *wants* a Dodge Charger Hellcat. We sometimes tell ourselves that we would be happier if we had the things we want, but I guarantee that we would then have new wants. Happiness is generally independent of these kinds of preferences.

Abraham Maslow is considered by some to be the father of humanistic psychology. His classic Theory of Human Motivation is portrayed as a pyramid, and at the top is the level of your best self or self-actualization.[6] At the bottom are the most basic physiological needs: food, water, and oxygen. Makes sense, right? If we don't have oxygen, we will not get very far. The next level is safety needs: bodily safety, shelter, and security. Again, it is kind of hard to imagine being your best self when you are more concerned with being safe. The third level is love and belonging: relationships with family, friends, and lovers. I'm thinking that things are starting to click now. Once we are safe, in order to be our best selves, we need to have a sense of belonging, companionship, and love. The fourth level is esteem: self-confidence, self-respect, and respect of others. This becomes a little more challenging. The fifth and final level is self-actualization, which is being your best self possible. Maslow didn't believe many people made it to this level.

Once you have enough money to cover basic needs, the relationship between money and happiness fades away. While it is sexy to tell oneself the story about how wonderful life would be with an endless supply of money, surely you have seen headlines about very rich people who have fucked up lives regardless of income. Some very wealthy people talk about giving away their money rather than leaving it to their kids because they realize that having too much money causes problems on its own.

There is something about having a gap between where we are and what we want that incentivizes us to push harder to reach our potential. Again, I am not talking about people who live in poverty or struggle with basic needs. I am talking about a point beyond this.

Stop telling yourself that you will be happy when you have more money, have a certain car, live in a certain neighborhood, have x, y, z, and on and on. There will never be enough money. Let's be honest. It's a treadmill to nowhere. The most important parts of life, money can't buy.

Money can't buy love or the authentic respect of others, and it cannot buy self-actualization. I think that there is the allure that it can. People falsely chase money, hoping that it will buy these things, but I am sure that you can think of wealthy people who are quite insecure, not self-actualized, and absolutely not happy. Alternatively, there are folks who have just enough money to live and are happy without excess.

When I think of success in life, I think of being happy. In fact, I can think of no greater success. If a person spends all of her time chasing money with no free time to enjoy it, is that happiness? I don't know about other countries, but in the United States, there is extraordinarily undue emphasis placed on money with the implication that happiness is included in the package. Sadly, that sets young people off on a journey in pursuit of money, always believing happiness is in the package deal. I hope that somewhere along the way, the lesson becomes obvious, but the greatest tragedy is realizing that you spent your life chasing something that didn't give you what you sought all along.

Don't Pathologize Normal

To paraphrase a famous song, there is something happening here. I am noticing more and more people coming to my office questioning normal tendencies as if they are deeply flawed. In the last five years, I have seen a spike in young people coming in and identifying as *mentally ill* without sufficient evidence. Other people come in wondering if something is *wrong* with them because they seemingly differ from other people in preferences or ways of being in the world. Still, others find themselves upset in upsetting situations and don't like being upset, even if there is a good reason. Therefore, they must have depression or an anxiety disorder. Absolutely everyone has ADHD. I am gleaning that it is likely a side effect of social media, but hear me loudly say that we need to stop pathologizing normal differences.

This first came to my attention many years ago when I regularly met people who believed they had bipolar disorder, which is actually kind of rare. When I asked why they believed they had this, they would give examples like this: When I wake up, I am in a good mood. By the end of the day, I am really grouchy, and my mood is up and down. When I ask more questions, it becomes obvious why they have emotional changes, but they somehow believe that their feelings should be pretty even all of the time. By this definition, having a range of emotional reactions is wrong when, in fact, that is how we are programmed.

People also try to label folks they have conflict with as bipolar as a means of somehow undercutting the other person's credibility. These days, I am hearing that everyone you don't like is a narcissist. While I get the allure, narcissistic personality disorder is also not that common. We all have elements of being self-centered, as I mentioned earlier. That is a universal attribute of being human, but that doesn't make a narcissist. What it does do is make us feel superior to label the person we don't like as pathologically flawed.

The most recent trend I am seeing is around attachment. If someone feels uncertain or insecure in a new relationship, they must have an attachment disorder. If someone feels insecure in any way, that, too, is an attachment disorder. Note: Feeling insecure in new social relationships is normal. It is healthy and expected. Being unhappy in difficult circumstances is a typical reaction. Each and every one of us has difficulty concentrating in a rapidly changing, overscheduled, and overstimulated world.

The fact of the matter is that evolution requires a diversity of traits. This means that not everyone is going to be wired or programmed the exact same way. Qualities are spread among people to increase the chances of survival. Differences are a good thing! Just because you find that you have an atypical reaction or style of being from your friends doesn't mean that you are pathologically flawed.

The vast majority of people do not have attachment disorders or bipolar disorder and are not narcissists. Overuse of these terms creates unnecessary anxiety and diminishes the complexity of actual diagnoses that deserve serious treatment.

I'm not quite sure if the desire to pathologize is a way to try and better understand or manage experiences or if it is a way to defend oneself against criticism from others. ("I can't help it that I'm insecure. I have anxious attachment.") I sometimes see diagnostic labels used as a way to fit in. People talk about their social groups where everyone has a diagnosis. They need one, too.

I object to this excess labeling and pathologizing. We have unique experiences and perspectives, and that is okay. We should be given a diagnosis only when our symptoms reach the threshold of being so culturally atypical that we aren't able to engage in healthy function or in social or work interactions. And keep in mind that these labels were historically used to stigmatize and undermine people's credibility. Never give people ammunition to challenge your standing in the world by calling you a medicalized name unless you need the name in order to get care. Anything less is just control.

The Bullshit Ends Here

Newsflash! Bullshit is everywhere! Watch where you step.

Seriously, we live in a world where bullshit is inescapable. Here's the trick: If you are on the lookout for bullshit, you can effectively evade some of it. Of all the boundaries, this one, perhaps, is the most fundamental. It underlies so many of the other topics.

Unfortunately, bullshit is hard to define, as it is a deeply personal topic. For some people, bullshit is drama. For others, it is any waste of time, and for others, it is bad behavior by others. Some of us see it everywhere. Others find it in specific areas of life. All I know is that it is out there—waiting to welcome you into a trap.

First, you have to wake up expecting the bullshit. This involves acceptance of bullshit as part of life, with some level of unavoidable exposure. Second, you set your bullshit tolerance level for a particular day. How much bullshit do you feel is acceptable? How much can you take, given other things going on? How much is baked into your schedule? How much is optional? How much sleep have you had?

The next step is making a plan for the bullshit. There is expected bullshit (as in meetings with rogue characters trying to impress one another or filling in free time on the agenda), and then there is the unexpected bullshit (like getting a flat tire, having the toilet malfunction, or dealing with someone eating your lunch from the breakroom refrigerator). You can plan only for the expected bullshit because there is no point in planning for what you don't know will happen. Once you have assessed the potential for bullshit in your day, you can do things like appropriately caffeinating, building in an exercise break or deep breathing, or having something fun planned to offset the toxicity. You can steel yourself before going into a meeting when you are certain it will likely run over and Paul will use all the time talking about his pet projects.

Because you have set your bullshit tolerance and know just how much you are willing to put up with, you should be prepared to draw the line with other bullshit. That means walking away, ignoring, or shutting down bullshit because, let's face it, you are entitled to protect yourself, as we have previously covered.

Resting bitch face or having a bitch aura is a great way to prevent some level of bullshit from reaching you. This involves creating visuals, body language, and general vibes for people to stay the fuck away from you. A colleague of mine taught me another cool trick. You start the day by announcing that you have a low bullshit tolerance. This actively communicates to others that they should take their bullshit elsewhere or face an unpleasant wrath. I am guessing there are fun little signs you can put by your desk to allow others to know the bullshit-o-meter for the day, although the risk is that you invite a certain level of bullshit when you indicate being open to any at all.

In the event these methods seem too overt, you may wonder how else to set boundaries around bullshit. You can tell someone to SWOT it out as previously covered (see page 135). You can feign illness or an emergency bathroom visit. You can preemptively weave into a potentially bad conversation that you are dealing with some emergency or home stress, like the dog being sick.

If you want a more lasting solution, let me share with you something I taught once to a person who had everyone stopping by her desk during the day to shoot the shit. Because this person was very kind and caring, the bullshit was drawn right to her, and she didn't know how to get rid of it. The consequence was that she could never get any work done, and frankly, she didn't want to hear any more bullshit. I told this person to say: "Hey, I'm sorry to interrupt, but today is super busy. I am worried I won't be able to get this project done." (NOTE: Do not say that you can talk later!) Or, "Gosh, I'm noticing that I am falling behind in my work. I've really got to get back at it." Follow this up with avoiding eye contact or being too friendly, and the behavior may be extinguished.

My personal trick is to make a pronouncement that I am mentally unwell. This is a loud and clear sign to those around me to get their act together. It works every time.

The bottom line is that boundaries around bullshit take effort. Sometimes you won't even see it coming, which is why you need to be preemptive in your expectations and toolkit supplies and be prepared regardless of the circumstances. I cannot emphasize enough how important it is to have an air of zero bullshit. This will convey to others that you are not a bullshit-safe person, and that is exactly what you want.

Power and Control Are Illusions

There is a fairy tale humans tell themselves. It goes something like, "One day, when I have [money, power, title, status], I will [punish others, make better choices, have a better life]." Mentally, I've also been there. In some respects, daydreaming about having power and control helps us cope with present adversity, but there is a downside. The grass is rarely greener, and we risk missing out on enjoying where we are in life.

Luckily, I am a keen observer of others and life, and I have a profession where I get to meet a lot of people and hear intimate details of their lives. This quiets my own escapist tendencies without ever having to experience the lessons myself.

I have learned that the more a person chases power and control, the more out of control life can become. True control is an illusion to begin with. We can feel in control, but it is mostly momentary and delusional. Shit happens all the time that we don't expect, don't see coming, and can't change. The more we try and lock something down, the more time we spend trying to keep it in line. The high of feeling in control is outdone by the low of the crash when we realize it is over.

Some people try to increase influence by chasing power. Similarly, the quest for authority comes at a great cost, and I tend to also see it as elusive.

I had a friend who had big ideas of becoming an executive with a title, a person with the power to make the big decisions. The drive behind wanting this was not evil. He wanted the power to make a meaningful difference, and he told himself that this would not be possible without status. I watched from the sidelines because my observation was that the higher a person moves up the ladder of status, the less power that person actually has. The rungs of the ladder come with more baggage that gets in the way of getting things done. When you don't have the status, you don't understand the baggage that comes with it, hence the illusion of control.

Higher status comes with increased visibility, more problems brought to your desk, more pressure to please parties with competing interests, higher consequences when things don't go well, more work, and less sleep. No. Thank. You.

Everything comes with a tradeoff. I am not saying that the drive to achieve is bad. Telling oneself that power and control can be had without ginormous sacrifices is a lie. Sometimes, you end up losing control over the most important things (like your life) and you end up feeling more out of control than ever, particularly when others are beating down your door to complain to the person in charge.

The least you can do is be honest with yourself. Those at the top of the scrap heap easily become preoccupied with trying to stay there and are less able to fix

the problems they saw at the bottom.

Do You See a Victim or Survivor?

One of the first lessons they taught in my counseling grad program was: Are you going to view the person in front of you as a victim or a survivor? This makes a big difference in how you communicate, how you treat the person, and the energy in the room. If I see a victim, I pity the person. I feel sorry for them. I am sure I convey a sense of sorrow, and as a result, I may inadvertently indicate that I think the person is weak or can't do. This also affects how I see myself because if I see a person as a victim who has consulted me, I must be powerful, knowledgeable, and resourceful. The resulting story I tell myself is that I can help save the person. I have the power. They do not.

Alternatively, if I view the person in front of me as a survivor, I see the person as strong and resilient. I look at them with awe and admiration. I focus less on what is wrong than what is right. I deeply understand that the person survived before she met me and would have survived had she never met me. I am merely a consultant or witness, not a savior, and my role is supportive. The expert is the person in front of me. I do not have the power. The other person has the power.

Maybe you are not a therapist. How does this apply to you? The way you view people is central to boundaries. If you view others as victims and weak, you will always feel the need to fix, rescue, and intervene without even reflecting on the *should* of the matter. Indeed, jumping in to save someone may not be in the person's best interest if that person can learn the skills to save himself. The lens through which you view others will tend to dictate your actions.

While I am a strong believer in community and helping others, I am an even stronger believer in allowing others the pride and accomplishment of helping themselves with support when possible. I choose not to see people as broken and damaged because I see it as degrading. I prefer to see people as hurt, demoralized, afraid, confused, or injured—but always stronger than they might feel. I see a survivor who might be ready to embark on the path of a thriver.

None of this means that I turn my back or ignore someone in pain. It does emphasize that my role is supportive and not savior-like. Maybe this makes it easier for me to sleep at night, but it also makes a huge difference in setting the tone.

Check yourself. Do you treat others as victims, or do you see other people as survivors? Who is being served by your mindset?

Get Your Face Off the Screen

Since I know you've heard this before, I won't belabor the point, but research is pretty darn clear that the more time we spend on technology, the more distress we have. It isn't just kids and teenagers, and it isn't just social media.

Look what happened during the lockdown of COVID-19: Anxiety, substance use, and overeating all went through the roof. Yes, I understand that the causes are multi-factorial. There were real concerns about death and disability, loss of income, and unpredictability. I do not, however, underestimate the impact of not having enough face-to-face people time, and many folks report that socialization still has not gotten back to baseline.

Our brains are wired to be in the presence of other humans. Think of it as a survival skill. In an apocalypse, we would be more likely to survive if we had other people to share with, rely on, and work together with. Other people have resources and skills that we don't have. Facetiming isn't a substitute.

Technology time includes social media, computer time, television time, and the like. These activities don't provide our brains with the connection to other people necessary to fuel energy, mood, and engagement. Instead, we feed a sense of isolation, loneliness, and disconnection. I do understand that some tech time is essential in our world, but set some limits, please. You may look up and find that time, experiences, and life have passed you by, and tech can never reciprocate the companionship you seek. It fills empty space, but it is empty space you need to get up and fill with life. This takes extra effort, and I get that it doesn't sound fun. Yet, it is in that work that we are actually living. That work and effort are life. Virtual is out. Real is in.

It's Time to Break Tradition

There is hardly a more stale comment than, "This is the way we have always done it." Talk about a soul crusher for people with ideas.

If we never deviated from past traditions, how would anything ever change? Where would innovation come into play? I get the concept *why change a good thing*, but what if there is something better or at least different? Is it not worth exploring?

Admittedly, I am a creature of habit, so I don't take this subject lightly. Traditions are comfortable. They are emotionally laden with nostalgia and memories. At the same time, doing something for comfort's-sake has a lot of downsides. The zone of comfort is also the sector of slow death, boredom, and waste. The zone of discomfort is a surefire way to get folks motivated to up their game.

A perfect example is the unexpected learning around COVID-19. We learned that we can effectively work from home—or can we? When we had to work from home, people learned how to navigate technology very quickly, and this was a good thing. There was some cool innovation. Then, folks decided that working from home was superior and suggested that it should be a mainstay. After a bit, a good chunk decided that returning to the office, at least part-time, was a perfect middle ground for engagement and productivity. While we are still in the middle of this playing out, the lesson from the pandemic is the importance of flexibility. Work can flex to meet the diverse needs of people and still be effective.

Next time you find yourself wanting to fall into the mindset of doing something just because it has always been done that way, remember that this is the path of decay. At the very least, take a second look. Ask for other perspectives. I think this might also fall under the umbrella of continuous quality improvement. You build on what you have with a perpetual eye on making it better. Fuck boring.

You are a rebel with a cause: being a better you.

Health, Hypochondriasis, and Throwing in the Towel

I am a health psychologist, so I like to talk about well-being and what we can do to promote healthy behavior. For years, we've studied motivators, behavioral predictors, and anything else we can think of to explain why people act in certain ways and make the decisions they do about health. Needless to say, it is complicated—very complicated. No one model best explains human behavior because human behavior is messy and affected by so many things all at once.

Because there are a multitude of ways to look at health-related behavior, I am going to take a middle-lane approach. Some of us out there are control *freaks*. We have anxiety. I absolutely count myself as an anxious control freak work-in-progress. Folks who have anxiety think about illness and health most of the time. Hypochondriasis is a badge many people, like me, wear. What I mean is that we focus a lot of energy and attention on what is going on in the body and easily become self-convinced that there is something wrong—it's just that the malady is yet to be discovered. Not only are we sure without evidence that we have cancer, heart disease, or some other condition, we become fixated on the idea. We see signs of it everywhere. Once we become assured by our healthcare provider that we are fine, we move on to the next health-related fear. It is a battle with the rabbit hole.

Here is the legitimate dilemma that underlies the fear of getting sick: We can do all of the right things for health—eat right, exercise, follow the physicians' guidance, use sunscreen, and so on—and still end up with diseases. I heartily acknowledge that this truth fucking sucks because those of us with control issues cannot fully come to terms with this reality even though we accept that it is true.

At the same time, there is an equally large group of people who think: *Oh well, bad health is in my genes. I can't do anything about it, so I will do nothing. I'm going to die of something anyway.* This is similarly self-defeating.

The uneasy peace is finding ways to make healthy choices that don't control our lives to the point of making ourselves sick or giving up completely to chance. We find a way to coexist with things we cannot control while maximizing things that we can. I can control not losing my mind with worry so that I lose sight of my health at this moment.

In general, Americans have persistently become more sedentary and habituated to processed, unhealthy food. In some cases, it is not obvious that we are actually eating food. It becomes harder and harder to find health within this existence. We increasingly look to medications, surgeries, and miracle cures to fix what we have not learned to change with behavior and choice. We have also moved toward positive acceptance of unhealthy states of being as a means to validate less-than-healthy choices. I am worried about this, which is not to say that I am not accepting of individual differences. I do not support fat shaming or ridiculing people for being weak-willed. I understand that there are a multitude of health behavior determinants, including access to healthy foods, knowledge, and financial factors. At the same time, I am all about expanding health promotion. We cannot continue to tout the validity of only the science that we want to believe. Anything less undermines all science.

I do not believe in extremes of any sort. I believe in moderation, middle lanes, and multiple modalities. I support a view of health broadly conceived, not a slim definition. This starts with an honest conversation, where facts can be shared without judgment. None of us may like that conversation, but I will begin by saying that ownership over one's own health in some form is part of the equation, and I don't say that in blame language. Ownership is about having an active role where the buck stops with you.

Health boundaries are focusing on what you can control and being open to learning and growth. They are about calling out perceived quick fixes that may leave you with another set of problems entirely. In the end, it is your body, and you only get one. I think this is called self-care for a reason.

Too Much of a Good Thing

This is another solid issue for me (and you now know that I have any just like you). I don't do one bite of pizza or one taste of cake because one nibble doesn't exist as a reality in my world. I can tell myself I will take a bite, but my self knows this is a fucking lie. I hate to lie to my self; she has my back. In this scenario, the decision is: Do I embrace the pain of not delighting in pizza or cake, or do I dive into self-indulgence with abandon? There is no middle ground, and I am willing to admit that.

The key to making my choice is the clarity that if I give myself free rein, I will certainly have a junk food hangover. That is, I will feel like trash later. Is it worth it? There is a good thing, and then there is a bit too much of a good thing. Sometimes it is better to walk away. Other times, there is perceived worth in embracing the sucky side effects of decadence. Again, the key is self-honesty.

There are lots of things in life where a little bit is fine, but too much is not so great. It is the dialing back that is an issue. I mean, if a little is good, a lot must be amazing, right? Or, not so much. I am sure we can all think of friends where a little goes a long way. The same goes for time off. A little feels luxurious. A lot feels boring, and we get sluggish and lazy.

The trick is knowing human tendencies. We habituate to things that are too familiar, like falling into habits of drinking too much or overloading on junk food. At the same time, if we over-restrict, it creates a drive to overindulge. See the problems?

To be successful, we have to find a lane of authenticity and intentionality around excess anything and figure out a way to experience pleasure without going overboard. Stop acting like you didn't know better when you chose to stay up all night binge-watching or playing video games. It's not new information.

The boundary is a reality check. We've been studying the brain and human behavior for decades, and we know a thing or two about the brain, motivation, health, and optimal performance. Yes, in an ideal world, we would be capable of superhuman choices. This world ain't that, and neither are you. Be aware of your choices. Make them deliberately, and do not lie about the consequences. Indulgence should be a treat, not a crutch for stagnation.

The Pity Party

We've all been to the pity party, probably more than a few times. We don't necessarily like it there, but we find ourselves going back. In fact, there are times that, like Denny's, we don't know how we got there, but that's where we ended up.

The pity party is the place of self-sorrow. There, we bemoan the injustice of it all. We wail about why things turned out such that we find ourselves there once again. Even though the pity party is serving shit sandwiches and we hate them, it is also self-indulgent. At the pity party, we feel righteous about deserving temper tantrums, tears, and slovenly behavior.

Darnell wanted to study nursing, and he wanted to go to a certain top-tier school. He worked his ass off, and... he didn't get into his school of choice. Darnell was devastated, as he hadn't even considered a plan B. He felt his life stopped at that exact moment, and he didn't care about anything, including his hygiene. Darnell refused social interactions; he lay on his couch binge-watching nothingness and eating trash. Darnell was so ashamed and humiliated. He couldn't face anyone and told himself his life was doomed to suck.

Self-pity is human and a normal part of grief. We are sad because something didn't go our way. We are disappointed. We are hurt. We grieve the loss of these things, and there needs to be a safe space for that melancholy. Hence, the pity party—meaning, self-pity is welcome there.

There is nothing wrong with actively attending or finding oneself at the pity party. The issue is how long you stay. There is no benefit to staying too long. It is sometimes good to go there, rest, center oneself, and rediscover strength. Staying too long, though, is like getting too much sun or drinking too much alcohol. It begins to impair or damage you. You get lethargic and have a hard time finding your way to the door.

Give yourself permission to feel bad when things don't go your way. You are human, after all, and it doesn't help to judge yourself for having human qualities. When you find yourself at a pity party, it's best to start eyeballing the door and finding someone who will drag you there if you lose sight of it—someone who can say, "Sister, I don't care where you go, but you can't stay here."

A Lonely Place Called Pride

We all have pride, and it isn't a bad thing. On the other hand, too much might be. When your pride gets in the way of apologies, opportunities, and moving on from the past, it becomes an obstructive issue. Pride won't make up for lost time or friendships or keep you warm at night. Pride can be a lonely place.

Dorothy was proud of her street smarts and work ethic. She was a high achiever, and she flaunted it at work. She enjoyed trash-talking with her colleagues about who was going to have the most impressive ideas at staff meetings. One day, Dorothy pitched her idea, and the team leader tore some pretty big holes in her presentation in front of everyone. Dorothy was humiliated. She seethed for the entire meeting and beyond. In fact, she went home for the day, feigning illness. She couldn't stand to face her coworkers after her perceived disgrace. The kicker was that another team member, Perry, had given her some helpful suggestions prior to that meeting that she had disregarded as inexperienced. Not only was Dorothy mortified by her public shame, but she realized that she owed Perry an apology. Given Dorothy's history of big talk, she decided she'd rather leave the job than apologize. She got on LinkedIn and immediately started looking for a new position.

Taking pride in one's work is having some skin in the game. It is personal investment. Having too much pride begins to interfere with growth because you can't learn anything with pride in the way. The opposite of pride is humility, a place of self-discovery. Humility is not self-effacement. It is not settling. It is approaching life with a beginner's mind and having a mindset that there is always something to learn. Feedback isn't seen as a personal attack or some sort of emotional abuse. It is welcomed as an opportunity to grow. We are all human with room to develop.

An overreliance on pride leads to defensiveness and reactivity because you always feel the need to refute any evidence that suggests a need for improvement. There is a whole different perspective you may be missing in the blinders of pride. As with most things in life, a little pride goes a long way.

Quick Fixes and Other Half-Assed Solutions

Even though I'd like to see myself as someone who would skip a quick fix in favor of a long-term solution, I would not be genuine if I told you I was. It's human to go for the immediate reinforcement.

Let's say that I was dumped by my partner, and I am heartbroken. I know that I need time alone to process my feelings and learn from the experience so I won't repeat some of the same mistakes. At the same time, being alone sucks: I cry all of the time, ruminate, and second-guess and gaslight myself. I am simply no fun. I have an idea! Why don't I start dating to get my mind off my ex? I know it isn't a good idea, but I am sure I will feel better. Feeling better is a good thing, right?

People do this all of the time. They choose the quick fix, which is to reduce pain or seek a thrill, over putting in the long-term work. I can save my money and buy something I want, or I can use my credit card and pay interest so I can have it now. Now is better, right?

Sometimes, we don't have a good choice. Maybe I have to buy something on my credit card in order to function well, but maybe I could have also been saving my money. The desire to choose the quick solution is human, but if quick resolutions are overutilized, they will only lead to more problems down the road. I would like to think that holding out for the long-term answer avoids having to repeat the same life lessons over and over. It is all about truthfulness and deliberation, recognizing the impulse to indulge, setting it aside, and making the best choice available.

Let me tell you about the Stanford Marshmallow Experiment. In 1972, Walter Mischel, a professor at Stanford, conducted a study with small children.[7] The kids were offered one marshmallow they could eat immediately, but if they waited a short period of time, they could get an additional marshmallow. They followed these children into later life. The children who delayed gratification or suppressed the impulse to immediately eat the marshmallow had more success on a variety of measures. Although scientists argue about actual predictive validity, I think there is something to be said about the value of patience. Choosing to resist the urge for quick satisfaction is associated with better outcomes in life.

I guess good things do come to those who wait (and work for it).

Too Much Empathy Is Self-Destructive

Empathy is the ability to imagine the experience of another person as if you were in that person's shoes. It is not possible to fully understand the experience of another, but it is imagining the actual experience and allowing the associated feelings to flow. Empathy is both a skill and a gift (or curse, depending on how you see it). What I mean is that empathy is a practice, and it takes effort for a lot of people. It is not necessarily easy, and it can be very draining.

There are people who identify as empaths, which I view as more of a talent or gift. Empaths can seemingly read the emotions of others without trying. They pick up on vibes, energy, emotions, and the experiences of others in a more intuitive way, even if they don't want to. It is not so much planned as automatic.

Vanya can walk into a room and immediately sense tension or discontent. She can sense if someone is upset or worried without the person saying a word. Vanya also has gut instincts that tell her whether or not to trust or stay in a situation. When someone starts crying, Vanya is also moved to tears. She is easily swayed to emotion by music and other artistic expression. Vanya is an empath.

Vanya views her empathic abilities as a double-edged sword. She loves being able to read and connect to others' emotions. At the same time, she often feels like she is losing a sense of herself as separate and independent. Empathy is incredibly challenging to control.

Empaths don't just have empathy for people they like. They have empathy for people who do bad things. Empaths can see and identify with life events that put someone in a position to make very immoral choices. Empaths can't help the connection, and it becomes quite easy to lose a sense of true north.

While empathy is an admirable ability, it must be managed in order to coexist with a healthy mindset. Of course, saying that doesn't make it easier. If I were offered the superhuman ability to read minds, I would not want it, despite the obvious allure. It would be too much information, and I might not know how to handle it. This is how I also see empathy. With any human quality, limits are a good thing, yet there is no toggle switch.

If you are an empath, it is okay to interrupt the connection. It is healthy to redirect yourself when you feel you are losing perspective. You can't help but pick up on the energy around you. You can, however, help how much time you spend mulling it over. This, too, is a skill to develop with practice. Just know that it is okay to look away.

I Hear You

I'm going to teach you a trick that has served me really well over the years. You probably aren't going to love it, but it works. Let me demonstrate.

Cha Cha was giving a presentation to the local parent and school association on some proposed school policy changes. The crowd was rough. The parents were vocal, and several were chronic complainers. What Cha Cha didn't want to do was get into an argument with a parent in front of everyone. The changes weren't especially controversial, but there was always at least one person who liked to argue. Cha Cha didn't want to appear defensive or closed off to discussion, but she also didn't want to escalate on the stage. At the event, Cha Cha gave her speech and took questions. When a parent challenged her, Cha Cha responded with, "That's a good point. I'm going to think about that," "Thank you for sharing," and "I don't have an answer for that, but I am going to do some digging."

When Cha Cha responded to provocations with acceptance, there was nothing left to argue. She was free to approach the parent personally to address lingering discussion (or not).

I think we get into a mindset of feeling the need to argue back, defend ourselves, and provide supporting evidence when sometimes we do not need to do so. The hard part is consciously assessing whether the need is real. Arguing back tends to be automatic.

When someone is trying to argue or challenge you and it isn't worth it, isn't the right time or place, or won't go anywhere, you can shut it down by saying, "I hear you," and nothing else, which leaves nothing to continue arguing about. You are also not saying that you agree or disagree. You aren't kowtowing. You are just saying you heard what was said.

When my teens give snarky feedback on my parenting skills, I typically respond, "Okay," and they *hate* it. I am neither affirming nor denying their opinion, and there is no need to prove myself. I am simply acknowledging they have been heard. When they see I am unfazed, the fun is over. There is no more oxygen for the interaction.

When I said you wouldn't love the technique, it is because most people feel unsatisfied with not seizing the opportunity to mount a defense or counterargument. I can only emphasize that the satisfaction of shutting down the argument and getting on with peaceful living kicks ass every damn day.

Assholery

Once I was at a party, and Kesha told a work story that many of us can relate to in some form. At Kesha's place of work, they'd had a community lunch the previous day, and there was leftover salad in one of those tin containers in the breakroom refrigerator. Kesha stopped in the breakroom to get a drink, and she found Roger eating out of the container *with his fingers*. Kesha paused in shock and retreated, not sure what to say. That is because one should never have to say to a coworker not to eat community food out of the container with their fingers.

If you have done this or eaten food that wasn't yours or borrowed food that wasn't yours, you have engaged in assholery. Assholery is defined, by me, as engaging in self-centered, rude behavior that you know (or should know) better than to engage in, but you do so anyway because you believe you can get away with it. Some other examples of assholery are:

- Bullying or making fun of others
- Taking credit for shit you didn't do
- Telling offensive or derogatory jokes at work, assuming the people around you share your sense of humor
- Talking down to people
- Behaving with entitlement
- Being abusive in words and behavior
- Using other people

If you find these behaviors apply to you, it is time to reign in the assholery because it is super annoying to folks who are forced to interact with you. Even though this book is about boundaries, people cannot always choose whose company to share. People need to keep food at work without concern that you are sticking your fingers in it because you know you can.

If you find that you are around people who engage in assholery, call that shit out. Kesha went back to her office and sent an office-wide memo outlining appropriate breakroom behavior, specifically telling people not to eat food from the refrigerator with their fingers. That is an appropriate boundary for an asshole.

The reason some folks struggle with how to respond to assholery is that they feel it is somehow rude to call out rude behavior. I am here to tell you that it isn't disrespectful because you wouldn't have had to if the other person had not acted like an asshole. While it may feel wrong to publicly call out inappropriate behavior, clearly the other person doesn't fully understand in a way that polite society does, so it's best to speak plainly. Tell these folks plainly to cut that shit out. No further explanation necessary. In some cases, you may smell assholery before it fully presents itself. In that case, it is completely fine to notify them that assholery will not be tolerated, i.e., don't try that nonsense here.

Group Think Is Yesterday and Boring

I'll let you in on a secret. The more diverse opinions there are in a group, the less likely the group will be misinformed or misdirected. Groupthink is a phenomenon among a group of people who all think alike. When decisions are made, there is no dissent because no one is seeing alternative perspectives. There is not enough diversity of experience, opinion, and background. Everyone sees issues the same way, and big things get missed as a result.

This is exactly why diversity in society is so important. We need the tension of people on different sides of an issue so that all sides are covered in moderation. It makes us stronger and more effective. It's evolutionary.

We all like to be around people who see the world the same as we do and hold themselves accountable for relationships, friendships, and interactions that push back against our experiences and world views. It is good for us and for the other person. Get out of the zone of safety. No growth happens there.

It takes work, and it will be uncomfortable because you will have to accept differences of opinion. You will say the wrong things. You will serve meat to vegetarians. You will have to ask questions. There may even be conflict. Why is that a bad thing if you are open to learning? You do not know what you are missing.

Just Do It

Here is a professional confession: I don't know how to help procrastinators other than to say, "Stop doing that." I understand why people procrastinate. It's often anxiety avoidance, meaning people avoid things because thinking about addressing them causes anxiety. So, they put off those things for another time, but there is, in fact, no good time to deal with anxiety-provoking issues.

Generally, there are two types of anxious people. There are anxiety approachers—the people who have anxiety and act impulsively to solve the issue. Then, there are the anxiety avoiders—those who think to themselves, *I will deal with that later*. While procrastination buys time, the anxiety associated with the unfinished task lingers in the back of your mind. The heaviness eats at you because you know the work still needs to get done.

I don't know of a magic trick that will fix this dilemma. There is a lot of clickbait on the internet claiming to have the answer. Confession: I've clicked, and they all say the same thing. Organize yourself. Develop goals. Set up a system to keep yourself on track. There is nothing new or magical because no miracle cure or silver bullet exists.

I only add that there is some benefit in reframing procrastination as an anxiety issue. Most folks I see sheepishly admit a tendency to procrastinate as if it were some kind of sin or referendum on worth. *Pshaw*. Seeing oneself as hopelessly flawed because you've labeled yourself as a procrastinator is not helpful. You then fall into a self-fulfilling prophecy. Instead, be real. Procrastination is avoidance of anxiety, and therefore, overcoming it is about finding ways to better manage anxiety. The sooner you deal with your anxiety, the better you will feel. No one can make you do this, though. You can use organizational skills. You can use goal setting. I have even seen some people procrastinate by making elaborate, color-coded plans to stop procrastinating. Procrastination prolongs the anxiety and pain. It may be more effective overall to first identify what is making you anxious and develop a strategy for managing that. The one thing we definitely know is that avoidance of anxiety does not work at all; it just puts it off for another day.

Set some limits on anxiety avoidance. Ask a friend to help. Set up rewards. Don't let yourself plan anything fun until it is done. Paradoxically, the cure is diving in. You know the saying: *Just do it*.

The Outside Package

Have you ever met someone who appeared visually stunning, but the more you got to know the person, the more ugly they appeared on the outside? I have, and I have also known people who were average in appearance but became stunningly attractive the more I got to know them. The outside package, despite what social media and other headlines tell us, is only one small part of you. Your adult self knows this. It's time for your emotional self to hear it, too.

More important than a person's external appearance is the inside package, qualities such as personality, intelligence, humor, kindness, adventurousness, trust, and loyalty. The inside package will either enhance or detract from the outside package. But here is the thing. The outside package will deteriorate over time no matter what you do. Age alone, if nothing else, changes how we look—often not in ways we prefer. At the same time, age seems to enhance the inside package, making us deeper, more interesting, and more value-rich.

Despite the advertising messages, influencers, and fake imagery of social media, we can reject the message of superficiality and remind ourselves that what really matters is inside. This is the stuff that can't be surgically altered or filled in. Granted, I would be a hypocrite if I said that I didn't attend to appearances. Appearances have a place. What I am suggesting is a boundary around too much emphasis on the exterior. Instead of chasing glory for qualities that we can't really help, how about equal or more time for those internal qualities that we are responsible for?

Mirror, mirror on the wall. Who's the kindest/smartest/funniest one of all?

Labeling Is for the Post Office

The human brain has some limitations, like wanting to categorize people and things. We typically don't like things that don't fit a category. All of this is merely for efficiency's sake so we can understand and remember. The problem is that not everything fits into our existing categories, and some things fit into multiple categories. While I get this as a cognitive organizational strategy inherent in the brain, it isn't super adaptive.

Take good or bad, right or wrong. These are categories, and it would be so helpful if we could easily fit our experiences into one or the other so life choices could be easy. Unfortunately, life doesn't work that way. I tell people there is often choice between shit and different shit. Choose your shit. We get into trouble when we tell ourselves things will be better over there or that this is good and that is bad. This is flawed thinking because it is labeling. In addition, when we get there, it doesn't look the same. What we thought was good really isn't as good. Does that make it bad? Is there a truly right versus wrong decision?

Let's say that we agree that murder is wrong. What if you murder a person who is trying to murder you? Let's say stealing is bad. What if you are stealing something that will save another person's life? Where do we draw the line? My proposition is that absolute labeling is the problem. There is an overall sense of right and wrong, but I don't know that there is absolute right versus wrong in every circumstance. There is only difference. We want to distill very complex experiences into simple categories because it makes us feel more comfortable or more sure. I propose to you that there is often no right or wrong in terms of the dilemmas we face. There just is. There is accepting the consequences of a decision in the moment based on what you believed was best given the information you had. The labeling, on the other hand, makes a moral judgment that may or may not be applicable in a strict sense.

This is also a great segue to mental health diagnoses. Not everyone who is selfish is a narcissist. Not everyone who says things you don't like is emotionally abusive. It is becoming viral in our society to slap a label on anyone who says or does things that we find upsetting. This is not healthy, productive, or accurate. If it were, we would all carry the labels at some point in time. In the 1960s, Dr. Thomas Szasz proposed that people were labeled as mentally ill as a means of social control. [8] While his views were a bit extreme, there has always been an element of truth to labeling as a way to slant the narrative. A few years ago, a member of the legislative branch in Michigan openly called out that state's female governor as "batshit," and don't think for a moment that this wasn't meant to create a storyline about her competence and stability.

Next time you find yourself labeling, clap back. Ask yourself if this is indeed reality or if you are trying to impose simplicity so you can sleep at night. How is the label helpful? Push back against labels about yourself. You are more than a label can ever adequately describe anyway.

When We Know How the Story Ends

When we are born, we don't have preconceived notions about ourselves, the world, and other people. Those notions are partially formed by our life experiences, specifically the way others treat us, which teaches us our place in the world and how things work. Our genetics shape how we view or filter those experiences. For example, if we have a genetic predisposition to doubt, worry, and fear, our life experiences will be viewed through the lens of anxiety. If we have a genetic predisposition to a pessimistic mindset, our experiences will be viewed through the lens of negativity. There is what happens in life, and then there is how we view what happens in life and what conclusions we draw.

Think of these life lessons as chapters in the story or narrative of us. Maybe our personal narrative is that we are likable, athletic, and social. On the other hand, we might have more self-defeating narratives, such as unlovable, unattractive, or unintelligent. I call these self-defeating narratives because the unhealthy stories we tell ourselves make us feel lousy. Because we believe them, we begin to enact them in our lives in ways that will not lead to our success. If we tell ourselves that we are unworthy, we feel unworthy. We may lower our standards, give up easily, or not try at all. It is a human tendency to cherry-pick information that confirms our beliefs and to discount data that contradicts those beliefs.

This may sound fatalistic, but it isn't at all. Once you become aware of self-defeating narratives, you can work to set them aside in your mind. In other words, you can set boundaries, edit the narratives, or create newer versions of them. This is what writers do as information evolves: They release updated, edited versions of prior works.

The original narratives, while they might still exist, do not have to automatically dictate your life perspective.

Once you are aware, you get to choose if you allow them to take over and dictate your behavior. It is entirely possible to edit them, ignore them, challenge them, and work around them.

You decide. You control. You have the power. Start with the boundaries in your head. How is what you are thinking helpful to what you want? Start writing counter-narratives. Time for a plot twist!

Why Not Just Be Aggressive?

Passive-aggressiveness is such a time waster. This personality trait or communication style is when people are not upfront about how they feel or what they want. They tend to say one thing, but because they don't really mean what they say, they behave in ways that contradict their words. For example, Sally knows that Rhonda doesn't like Peter. Sally and Rhonda are going to a concert, and Sally asks if Peter can come, acknowledging that Rhonda may not want him to be there. Sally tells Rhonda it is okay if she says, "No." Rhonda says, "Yes," and plans are made. At the last minute, Rhonda starts throwing in roadblocks to Peter coming, like there isn't enough room in the car, and there is no time to pick him up.

This is passive-aggressive. It is when someone isn't honest about how they feel, and it ends up sabotaging things later. Passive-aggressive communicators often say that they didn't feel safe to be honest or that they were afraid. This is a cop-out. Grow up. If someone asks you for input, give that person the courtesy of being honest. Decisions are being made, and those decisions depend on valid data. I would much rather have someone say something I prefer not to hear than spend time planning something that will be disrupted later.

It's kind of a shell game. You think you are dealing with one thing, only to be surprised later to find out that it is something else. So much time and energy would be saved just by knowing the facts upfront.

If you tend to be passive-aggressive, speak up! Give yourself permission to be honest about how you feel, whether you are asked or not. Put some skin in the game. You may tell yourself that you don't have the space to be honest for fear of rejection or discomfort, but those are restrictions you are placing upon yourself. Think of it as merely delaying the inevitable, which will come out later.

If you have passive-aggressive people in your life, call that malarky out. Create a norm where honesty is valued, and never attack someone for being honest after you asked them for honesty. That's the best way to ensure that they'll never be authentic again.

Dispense with the unnecessary bullshit. Life is already full of unavoidable asshattery. Don't add to it with passive-aggressiveness or tolerating it from others.

Understanding and Other Rabbit Holes

The allure of analyzing why other people do what they do is a humongous rabbit hole. The reason a lot of people fall into it is that they have an almost irresistible desire to understand or explain bad behavior, as if an explanation exists that will make such behavior digestible.

Sirisha is distraught that her boyfriend, Todd, leers at other women. She told him it bothers her, but he still does it. Sirisha entertains why he ogles in obsessive detail. She first thought it was because she wasn't sexy enough, but they had a vigorous, enjoyable sex life. She dressed in sexier outfits, but nothing changed. Sirisha then thought it was because she didn't give him enough attention, so she increased her focus. Nothing changed. She thought he didn't understand the intensity of her discontent, so she had *another* confrontation about his behavior. He expressed understanding and continued his inappropriate staring.

Sirisha went to counseling to ask a professional if Todd had attachment issues.

Even if Sirisha had an explanation for Todd's disturbing behavior, it would not change the fact that Todd is choosing to behave in ways that are upsetting to her. Her understanding does not change Todd or the situation. The lie is that Sirisha tells herself that if she understands, she can fix it, yet it is not hers to change.

Don't get me wrong. Some things we can better understand, like why we can't sleep at night or why we are sad all the time. For other issues, we will never have conclusive data, and continuing to seek it will only get in the way of forward progress. We fall into rabbit holes like this all the time, both with others and with ourselves. We persistently wonder why we engage in self-defeating behavior, why we prefer to be in control, and why we are activated by certain people. These are questions that we may never have definitive answers to, and still, we persist in the pursuit of elusive knowledge.

With Sirisha and Todd, her understanding of *why* Todd leers is irrelevant to his changing. He doesn't want to change, or he would seek help in doing so. Her preoccupation with an explanation perhaps helps her tolerate him more—telling herself that there is a valid reason to justify it all away.

If you find yourself jumping from explanation to explanation, you are probably circling down the rabbit hole, but be assured the answer is not there. Choose whichever rationalization you like best and move on. Focus on the behavior, which is measurable, changeable, and knowable.

Money, Gifts, and Loans

Finances are a touchy subject for most people. In fact, it is among the top three issues married couples fight about. The topic is laden with issues like fear, control, and embarrassment, as well as values like freedom and identity. It is no wonder that boundaries around financial issues are emotional landmines.

There is no easing into this one. Conversations about money need to be had early. If some friends enjoy expensive excursions and you are invited on one, don't let awkwardness get in the way of stating your concerns and needs. You don't get to dictate what the group does, but you can propose alternatives. You can authentically say that you feel fine bowing out of certain activities, or you can explain why you aren't going. Be prepared for how you will handle someone offering to pay your way, which is entirely fine if you are okay accepting, but don't take a loan if you don't want to spend the money.

If you plan a dinner with someone who chooses an expensive place you cannot afford, say so. Don't go and starve or be so consumed with worry that you don't enjoy the experience. And try to be sensitive to the needs of your friends when you are in the position of making suggestions. Don't assume. Ask and give permission for honesty. It relieves so much pressure.

While we're on the subject of honesty, if you don't want to be in gift exchanges, say so. Whether it is for the holidays or birthdays, it is completely acceptable to opt out. Personally, I don't like gift exchanges because I don't like to accumulate stuff. I am on a mission to minimize, and the thought of hauling more stuff home makes me feel heavy. Truly, no one wants to spend a bunch of time looking for a gift for you that you won't appreciate anyway. What a time-saver.

And, I'm sure you've heard this before, but don't lend money. If you do, there is such a large chance you won't see it again that you should consider it an unspoken gift. That way, you will not be excessively disappointed when you don't see the money again. Personally, I think it is a bad practice to lend money because it often leads to resentment when you see the other person spending in ways you judge to be reckless. I don't recommend it.

Boundaries around money will be as challenging as addressing conflict head-on. Your adult self knows they are good, but your child self will prefer to avoid them. You just have to establish them to become more comfortable. Get out of fantasy land. Be real with yourself, and make decisions that are in your best interest rather than trying to please or impress others.

Interesting how you can't get rich quick, but you can absolutely get poor in a heartbeat.

Let's Get Real

I'm not gonna lie. This lesson is personal. I despise lying. In my practice, I choose not to treat certain disorders because I understand that they come with covering up, loose truths, and outright lying. I simply cannot work with that. I choose to believe whatever people tell me as the truth because I don't have the time, energy, or desire to doubt it. Lying feels like a tremendous time-waster, and I am perhaps a little preoccupied with efficiency. I own it.

Lying is avoidance of that which is hard. Lying is procrastination. It is inauthentic. If I want to spend time in an alternative reality, I will watch a streaming mini-series. I view lying as a detour back to childhood imagination, where life could be what we dreamed up. If you are reading this book, I will assume that you are an adult and developmentally past that stage. You can tell yourself you are lying to save someone else's feelings, but this is also an untruth. You are being deceitful to save yourself the distress of confronting hard truths.

If life is to feel successful, we all have to grow up and face hard realities. That is the only way we can set about changing those realities to better fit what we want. None of this involves lying. Pain will inevitably be part of this. Lying is merely evasion and, in fact, harder in the long run because not only do you not get anything real done, but you carry a heavy burden of knowing that you are insincere.

Be braver than this. Step up. Be real. See that what you dodge is bigger in your mind than it ever was in reality. Overcome the fear. I promise you will feel a sense of relief that will set you free.

Light That Bitch on Fire

Gaslighting is what happens when others engage in manipulation tactics aimed at making you feel like you are losing your mind. It is meant to control you and is also a form of abuse.

Mitch had been dating Shane for a few months when he started noticing some red flags. Shane had always been a flirt, but now he was starting to seductively chat up other people right in front of Mitch. Whenever Mitch brought this up, it ended in a big fight. Shane would tell Mitch to check himself because jealousy was ugly on him. Shane brought up Mitch's past relationships, including intimate details Mitch had shared about being cheated on and having trust issues. He insisted Mitch was projecting his past insecurities onto him. He told Mitch to get therapy and work on his controlling nature and trust issues. Mitch would start the arguments feeling justified, but after Shane was through talking, he would doubt his own perceptions.

He began to think that maybe he was the cause of the problems after all and was overreacting. He thought this until he caught Shane making out with someone else at a party.

People gaslight to throw you off course. They don't like what you are saying, so they either subtly imply or flat out say that your experiences are not real or are made up. Expert gaslighters use details about your past against you to amp up your self-doubt. Because these personal details from your past provoke an emotional response, you become entangled in your own emotions and have a difficult time pursuing your complaints with vigor and righteousness. You begin to wonder if you have actually distorted reality.

Gaslighting is not when someone disagrees with you and refuses to accept responsibility for your concerns. Nor is it when others simply dispute your version of the truth or blame or attack you. So, be careful of calling anything you don't like to hear "gaslighting." It's more insidious than that. Gaslighting is someone using manipulation and power to influence your thoughts and feelings to the point that you wonder if you are losing your mind. It is others telling you that your concerns aren't reality-based.

People who love you in a healthy way don't gaslight you. People who love you listen and reflect. While they may disagree with your remarks, they are willing to apologize for any confusion or miscommunication. They care about how you feel and don't intentionally try to make you feel worse. If people gaslight you, run. Don't walk. It is not okay. You deserve better.

The Last Word

While this section may strongly resonate with parents in particular, I'm guessing thats the strong desire to have the final word in a disagreement is something we've all struggled with from time to time. True wisdom, however, is knowing when to divert from the road to nowhere. I deeply understand those alluring and tempting moments when we seemingly can't resist having the last word in a skirmish, but when does it end? Having the last word is more about one's ego or pride than it is about adding real value to a conversation.

At my house, some conversations with teens have gone something like this:

Me: "I don't like your tone of voice. Stop yelling."

Them: "You started it."

Me: "No, you started it."

Them: "No, you started it."

Me: "I only responded to you."

Them: "Leave me alone."

Me: "I will when you do your work."

Them: "I will do my work when you leave."

Me: "No, you won't. You haven't."

Them: "Because you are here. You need to stop."

Me: "No, you need to stop."

Them: "Stop."

Me: "That's what I said."

This is the conversation to nowhere. I could see this, and yet, I still engaged. Why do humans do this?

Maybe the last word is to get the goat of the person you are squabbling with. Getting the last word may be a show of power, an attempt to control how the interaction ends, but it is kind of an acknowledgment of powerlessness.

There is more power in knowing you walked away on your own terms. George Bernard Shaw conjured this scenario with a perfect image: "Never wrestle with a pig,"

he wrote. "You both get dirty, and the pig likes it."

The End

Look at you—all learned about boundaries and shit! Don't be greedy. It is time now to teach others. Wait a minute, though. I am not talking about helping others learn to set boundaries because you already know this is not about fixing other people, right? Similarly, I am not giving permission to violate others by pointing your finger with unsolicited advice and judgment.

Newsflash—I am talking about communicating to others around you that you have changed your boundaries. Show others where your boundaries are.

You cannot expect people around you to read your mind or understand your boundaries any more than you did before you read this book. Those around you won't automatically discern your thoughts or transformation. In fact, the first response of people close to you will likely be to feel threatened. Change is scary for a lot of people, but that doesn't make it a bad thing.

You can share the good news that self-care and self-protection are not luxuries but values that you are working to manifest through boundaries. If there are relationships you hope to keep, I encourage you to tell the people involved that you are making some changes to be healthier and happier. It will help folks who automatically jump to the conclusion that they have done something wrong or that you are checking out of the relationship. Upfront communication is about avoiding misunderstanding. If the relationships are worth maintaining, people will respect you for clear boundaries.

If reading this book has caused you to reflect and you recognize that you need more help making boundary-setting a reality, consider professional counseling. You can go to PsychologyToday.com to check out profiles of professionals in your area. Also, check out locator.apa.org or helpstartshere.org for additional leads. There is no better investment than your growth and wellness.

I love this quote by Sarah Eisenberg, LMSW: "Boundaries aren't rules that govern other people's behavior. They're promises you make to yourself." Here's to making and keeping those promises.

References

1. Seligman, Martin E. P. *Authentic Happiness: Using the New Positive Psychology to Realize Your Potential for Lasting Fulfillment*. New York: Free Press, 2004.

2. Rotter, Julian B. *Social Learning and Clinical Psychology*. Prentice-Hall Psychology Series. New York: Prentice-Hall, 1954.

3. Frankl, Viktor E. *Man's Search for Meaning*. Englewood Cliffs, NJ: Prentice Hall, 1970.

4. Knight, Sarah. *The Life-Changing Magic of Not Giving a F*ck: How to Stop Spending Time You Don't Have with People You Don't like Doing Things You Don't Want to Do*. New York: Voracious, 2015.

5. Shariatmadari, David. "A Real-Life Lord of the Flies: The Troubling Legacy of the Robbers Cave Experiment." *The Guardian*, April 16, 2018, sec.

Science.
https://www.theguardian.com/science/2018/apr/16/a
-real-life-lord-of-the-flies-the-troubling-legacy-of-
the-robbers-cave-experiment.

6. Maslow, Abraham. *"A Theory of Human Motivation."* Eastford, CT: Martino Fine Books, 2013.

7. Mischel, Walter, and Ebbe B. Ebbesen. "Attention in Delay of Gratification." *Journal of Personality and Social Psychology* 16, no. 2 (October 1970): 329–37. https://doi.org/10.1037/h0029815.

8. Szasz, Thomas S. *The Myth of Mental Illness: Foundations of a Theory of Personal Conduct.* New York: HarperCollins, 1961.

17207239R00203